MURDER MYSTEI

C000139586

P1   DEATH OF A CANARY: loosely adapted ～～ ...～.～. ～y ɔɔ Van Dine. Canary O'Dell has been brutally murdered. A room full of guests, one of whom is the murderer. Can Inspector Markham solve the mystery? Can Canary's sister, Miss Jane O'Dell, assist Markham with his enquiries?

P34   AN ENGLISH MURDER: loosely adapted from the novel by Cyril Hare (rights via AP Watts, 29 John St, London WC1N 2DR). Warbeck Hall. Winter 1951. Guests gather for Christmas. There is a raging snow-storm outside and the house is cut off from the outside world. A death occurs, then another, then another. Is it murder? If so, who is the killer?

P72   DEATH ON THE FRINGE: loosely adapted from a play by Sir Richard Parsons (performing rights via Sir Richard Parsons). We are in the world of fringe theatre, dictatorial directors, precious playwrights and luvvie actors. We are also in the world of murder and deceit.

Welcome to a series of classic murder mystery plays. The way each play is performed is simple. A murder is committed, actors interrogate suspects, the murderer is unmasked.

All guests have to do is guess the murderer's identity and work out how the killing occurred. Oh, and they also have to cast themselves as suspects, reading from prepared scripts!

Murder Mysteries Vol 2

DEATH OF A CANARY by John Dunne loosely adapted from the novel by SS Van Dine

Characters
Inspector Markham
Miss O'Dell
Police Sergeant
Amy Gibson
Bill Jessup
Charles Cleaver
Lucinda Lindquist
Sarah Spotswoode
Lewis Mannix
Tony Skeel
Alys la Fosse

Canary O'Dell has been brutally murdered. A room full of guests, one of whom is the murderer. Can Inspector Markham solve the mystery? Can Canary's sister, Miss Jane O'Dell, assist Markham with his enquiries?

Murder Mysteries Vol 2

ONE

THERE IS A LOUD SCREAM

ENTER INSPECTOR MARKHAM WHO CALLS ORDER

MARKHAM. Ladies and gentlemen. Do not be alarmed. My name is Inspector Markham. There has been a murder - the worst and ugliest I've seen in years. A young lady called Canary O'Dell has been strangled in her bedroom.

ENTER MISS O'DELL

O'DELL. Inspector, is it true about my sister?

MARKHAM. I'm afraid so, Miss O'Dell.

O'DELL. This is terrible.

MARKHAM. Were you and your sister close?

O'DELL. I really don't see -

MARKHAM. She was called Canary, an unusual name.

O'DELL. She once tried to break into show business. Someone told her she sang like a canary. It sort of stuck.

MARKHAM. Until someone decided to throttle her!

O'DELL. What information do you have on my sister's death, Inspector?

MARKHAM. Your sister was grabbed suddenly from behind and strangled. And she was robbed. All her rings and jewellery were stripped off her hands.

O'DELL. It must have taken a pretty strong man to strangle her so easily.

MARKHAM. Not necessarily. A woman driven to rage can have the strength of ten men.

O'DELL. Has a doctor been called?

MARKHAM. Our forensic people are examining the body right now.

O'DELL. Where was she found?

MARKHAM. In her room! It's as if a bomb's hit it. Ransacked and wrecked.

O'DELL. How dreadful!

MARKHAM. *(Picks up a document case and a jewel box)* And as for evidence, we have two items of interest. One's a document case. The other's a jewel box. As you can see, the document case is empty. The jewel box, however, has been violently wrenched open –

O'DELL. By what, do you suppose?

MARKHAM. *(Picks up a nearby knife)* By this knife!

O'DELL. That puny knife never opened this jewel box. The knife might have twisted the box a little, but it never snapped open the lock.

MARKHAM. *(Looking around)* What are all these people doing here?

O'DELL. They're all friends of my sister.

MARKHAM. Well, nobody here can leave. My men will need to question them all. They may be material witnesses to the crime.

O'DELL. I wouldn't guarantee this lot being material to anything. Do you mind if I help? I do have a vested interest.

MARKHAM. Not at all! I shall need all the help I can get on this case. Now, where is the doctor's report?

ENTER THE SERGEANT WITH THE DOCTOR'S REPORT

MARKHAM. Ah, Sergeant, at last. *(Reads the report)* As I suspected, it's a simple case of strangulation from behind. Attack must have been unexpected. A quick competent job, though the deceased battled a little -

O'DELL. Was my sister sexually -

MARKHAM. Active?

O'DELL. No, assaulted.

MARKHAM. Whatever the motive was, it wasn't carnal!

O'DELL. What about the time of death?

MARKHAM. Mid afternoon - between two and three! Not much to go on, I admit.

O'DELL. What about the forensic report?

MARKHAM. That's here as well. My sergeant can be pretty thorough – when the mood takes.

O'DELL. Anything on the jewel box?

MARKHAM. Two instruments were used to open the jewel box. One bent the lid and the other actually broke the lock. The first instrument was employed amateurishly. But the other, possibly a steel chisel of some sort, was inserted with an expert knowledge.

O'DELL. A professional job, then?

MARKHAM. Highly so!

O'DELL. *(Doubtful)* I'm not sure about the jewel box, Inspector?

MARKHAM. What is there not to be sure about?

O'DELL. The murderer obviously tried the knife first, and then, finding it wouldn't work, tried a chisel. If he'd had an efficient chisel in the first place, why waste time using a knife? It doesn't make sense.

MARKHAM. Never mind about the knife. We have witness reports to consider.

O'DELL. There is one thing I should draw your attention to before you start interviewing people. And that's the matter of entrances and exits to the hotel – and my sisters' room especially. All the windows at the hotel are equipped with security locks. Now, there's only one entrance to my sister's room, and that's the door leading off the main hall. That means that the only way that anybody can get in or out of her room is through the front door.

MARKHAM. Isn't there a side door?

O'DELL. There is, at the end of the passageway. It's the only side or rear entrance to the hotel. But the door is bolted – on the inside – (not locked, mind you, but bolted) which makes it impossible for anyone to enter the place, except by the front entrance.

MARKHAM. This complicates things somewhat. There're only two ways into the hotel. The hall, or through a side door, which is bolted from the inside. I would therefore appreciate someone telling me how your sister's little playmate got into her room this afternoon. And I'd also like to know how they got out.

O'DELL. It must have been through the front door. It's the only logical way.

MARKHAM. Tell me, did you and your sister get on well?

O'DELL. Oh, we got on all right. We were never that close, that's all.

MARKHAM. Maybe I should check your alibi while we're about it.

O'DELL. Who actually found my sister's body?

MARKHAM. A woman called Amy Gibson. She and your sister were friends. She had a key to your sister's room. I think we should speak to Amy Gibson.

ENTER AMY GIBSON

MARKHAM. Ah, Amy, please tell us exactly what happened.

GIBSON. I arrived at Canary's room about three o'clock. I knocked. There was no answer, so I let myself in. As soon as I opened the door, I saw the mess - I also spotted the body of poor Canary. I called Bill Jessup at once –

MARKHAM. Bill Jessup?

GIBSON. Bill's been hanging around reception for most of the day. He's supposed to have organised this evening's little do. He wanted to make sure everyone arrived okay.

MARKHAM. Please, tell us what happened.

GIBSON. He came and we immediately notified the police. We then waited for the authorities to arrive.

MARKHAM. So, when did you last see Miss Canary?

GIBSON. This morning! She was fine. She was going out to lunch with a friend.

MARKHAM. Was this friend male or female?

GIBSON. A woman! I don't know her name.

MARKHAM. Did Miss Canary anticipate any danger, or have any fear of her companion?

GIBSON. Not at all, she was in good spirits.

MARKHAM. Do you know what jewellery Miss Canary wore today?

GIBSON. I think she wore all her rings, five or six of them, and three bracelets.

MARKHAM. Could anyone have been hidden in her room when you left?

GIBSON. Where could anyone hide?

MARKHAM. There are several possible places. In the wardrobe for a start!

GIBSON. Why would anyone want to hide in a wardrobe?

MARKHAM. Do you know of anyone Miss Canary was in the habit of going out with?

GIBSON. Canary was very careful about who she saw - secretive, you might say.

MARKHAM. And you never heard her speak of anyone of whom she was frightened - or anyone she had reason to fear?

GIBSON. No - although there was one man she was trying to get rid of. I wouldn't have trusted him anywhere. I told Canary she'd better look out for him. But she'd known him a long time and had been pretty soft on him once.

MARKHAM. How do you happen to know this?

GIBSON. One day, about a week ago, I came in after lunch and he was with her in the bar. They didn't see me. He was demanding money and when she tried to put him off, he began threatening her. I then made a noise and they stopped arguing. And pretty soon he left.

MARKHAM. What did this man look like?

GIBSON. He was kind of average - not very tall.

MARKHAM. Strange, you having a key to Miss Canary's room.

GIBSON. I'm afraid many people did. Canary was trusting that way.

MARKHAM. Thank you. That will be all. This Bill Jessup, do ask him to join us.

AMY GIBSON EXITS. ENTER BILL JESSUP

MARKHAM. Mr Jessup. I understand you were here for most of the day.

JESSUP. I was. What of it?

MARKHAM. Did you see Miss Canary come in after her lunch appointment?

JESSUP. Yes. I had to answer the door to everyone.

MARKHAM. Unusual for you to be there for most of the day!

JESSUP. I had a responsibility to make sure everyone arrived on time.

MARKHAM. I see. What time did Canary arrive?

JESSUP. It couldn't have been more than a few minutes after two.

MARKHAM. Was she alone?

JESSUP. No, there was a woman with her. I don't know her name.

MARKHAM. Did she accompany Miss Canary into her room or did she leave immediately?

JESSUP. She went in with Canary and stayed for about half an hour, then left. But she came back after ten minutes or so, saying she'd forgotten her phone.

MARKHAM. So, this woman arrived about two and was alone with Miss Canary in her room until about half past. Did anyone else call on Miss Canary at any time today?

JESSUP. There was only one person that called -

MARKHAM. Oh, really. When was this? And what happened?

JESSUP. It was about twelve o'clock. Canary had already left for lunch. She was a young woman. I don't know her name. She insisted on coming in and walked down the hall. I told her Canary wasn't in. But she kept on going. She knocked on the door, but of course there wasn't any answer. So she left.

MARKHAM. You actually saw her go out?

JESSUP. She stopped just outside the front door and lit a cigarette. Then she left.

O'DELL. One by one the rosy petals fall.

MARKHAM. And no one else visited Miss Canary?

JESSUP. I would have seen them. They would have had to pass me in order to reach Canary's room.

MARKHAM. And you never left the hall.

JESSUP. There was something else. When the lady came out of Canary's room the second time, she stopped and asked me to ring for a taxi. While she was waiting for the taxi, Canary screamed and called for help.

MARKHAM. Ah! Something to work on!

JESSUP. We all rushed to Canary's door. The lady knocked, but there was no answer. Then she knocked again and at the same time called out to Canary. This time Canary did answer. She said *"Nothing is the matter! I'm sorry! Everything is all right! Please go home! And don't worry!"* Then we all walked back to the hall. The woman remarked that Canary must have dozed off and had a bad dream. We chatted for a few minutes and then the taxi came. She said good-bye and went out and I saw the car drive away.

MARKHAM. How long was it after this woman came out of the room that you heard Miss Canary scream?

JESSUP. A few minutes!

MARKHAM. You could hear her plainly through the door then?

JESSUP. Oh, yes.

MARKHAM. Did you hear any other suspicious sounds in Miss Canary's room?

JESSUP. Not a sound. However, someone from outside the building telephoned Canary. We have a switchboard here.

MARKHAM. What's this?

JESSUP. About twenty to three someone telephoned Canary.

MARKHAM. Thank you, that will be all.

BILL JESSUP EXITS

O'DELL. It doesn't make much sense. The murderer got in some way and got out too. There's something wrong somewhere. Either Amy Gibson is mistaken about someone being in my sister's room when she left or else Bill Jessup left the hall and won't admit it.

MARKHAM. Amy Gibson seems trustworthy enough. And if there was any doubt about anyone having come in the front door unnoticed, Bill Jessup would be only too eager to admit it.

O'DELL. So, what we need now are a few suspects. Perhaps your general enquiries will throw something up.

MARKHAM. What we really need is the name of the woman who took your sister to lunch today.

O'DELL. And we need to know the names of all the people my sister was seeing.

MARKHAM. And we still have all these people to contend with.

O'DELL. Perhaps they can help with your enquiries.

MARKHAM. And we still have the matter of your alibi.

O'DELL. My alibi can be checked easily enough. I work for a second rate theatre company. I've been rehearsing all day. A murder mystery play! A dreadful script!

THEY EXIT

TWO

ENTER MARKHAM AND O'DELL

MARKHAM. We've got the woman who took your sister to lunch today. A lady by the name of Sarah Spotswoode! She has also been seeing your sister a good deal - if you take my meaning.

O'DELL. I knew my sister led a colourful life -

MARKHAM. Your sister's sex life was entirely her own concern. Spotswoode took your sister out to lunch today. She's actually quite disconcerted. She's afraid her connection with your sister will leak out and disgrace her.

O'DELL. And will it?

MARKHAM. I hardly see the necessity. No one knows who your sister's escort was today and if this woman has nothing to do with the crime, what's to be gained by dragging her into it? As long as she tells us the whole story - I daresay her account of the day will agree with Bill Jessup's.

O'DELL. So where did Sarah Spotswoode go after leaving here?

MARKHAM. After she left here she drove into town and, arriving at about ten past three, met with some friends who insisted she joined them for a coffee.

O'DELL. At least her coming forward closes one line of inquiry. Perhaps we should check up on her alibi.

MARKHAM. We've already phoned her friends. They verify her statement.

O'DELL. Anything else?

MARKHAM. We have news on the condition of the jewel box we found in the bedroom. Apparently the box was prised open with a chisel. It was an old instrument - there being a particular nick in the blade. And furthermore, it was the same one used in a successful housebreak early last summer.

O'DELL. If that's the case, why did this experienced burglar first use an insufficient knife?

MARKHAM. Forget the knife. The murderer wrenched the box open with a steel chisel and that same chisel was used last summer in another burglary. That makes this a professional job.

O'DELL. That's what bothers me, Inspector.

MARKHAM. We've got further news on your sister. From what we understand, she didn't run around with too many people - she limited herself to a few live wires and played the game with what you'd call *finesse*. The principal one is a man called Charles Cleaver.

O'DELL. Anyone else in the frame?

MARKHAM. There's a fellow named Lewis Mannix. He first met your sister when she was an actress -

O'DELL. We don't talk about those years.

MARKHAM. But she chucked him over a year ago and they haven't been seen together since. His affair with your sister went cold too long ago. So we eliminate him.

O'DELL. If you eliminate too many people, you won't have anything left but my sister's corpse.

MARKHAM. We still have Sarah Spotswoode.

O'DELL. Anything else to report, Inspector?

MARKHAM. A lead on the fingerprints! We lifted a few prints and, get this, a clear print on the inside of the wardrobe door. And better still, they were made by a certain Tony Skeel. Skeel's a known criminal and an artist in his line. I'd say he's our man - he's got a record as long as your arm. I think we should question him.

O'DELL. Fine!

MARKHAM. And yet -

O'DELL. And yet what?

MARKHAM. Tony Skeel may have ripped open the jewel box but his head isn't the right shape for the rest of today's performance.

O'DELL. Perhaps we should interview some of our other suspects. Let's start off with this Charles Cleaver character. I understand he's here this evening.

ENTER CHARLES CLEAVER

MARKHAM. I'm sorry to trouble you, Mr. Cleaver, but as you've probably heard, a young woman by the name of Canary O'Dell was murdered here. In making enquiries into her affairs I learn that you, among others, were fairly well acquainted with her. And knowing this young woman as well as you did, you are no doubt in possession of certain facts which would throw light on her brutal murder.

CLEAVER. I'm afraid I can't accommodate you.

MARKHAM. So you say. But your help would be appreciated all the same.

CLEAVER. I can eliminate myself easily enough. I was booked for speeding - today - at two thirty. Got myself caught on the motorway. Damn nuisance. I had to go and pick my brother up from the airport. He's staying with me.

MARKHAM. Just tell me what you know.

CLEAVER. I liked Canary. In fact, I was pretty much attached to her at one time. Did a number of foolish things, wrote her a lot of letters for one thing. Then she began to get cool and distant. Broke several appointments with me! I raised the devil with her but the only answer I got was a demand for money.

MARKHAM. Are you saying she blackmailed you?

CLEAVER. There's no use lying about it. She had those letters and she touched me for a neat little sum before I got them back.

MARKHAM. When was this?

CLEAVER. Last June. Look, I don't want to throw mud at a dead person, but that woman was the shrewdest blackmailer it's ever been my misfortune to meet. And I'll say this, too - I wasn't the only easy mark she squeezed. She had others on her string. I happen to know she once dug into old Lewis Mannix for plenty -

MARKHAM. Do you happen to know of another man she was interested in - name of Tony Skeel?

CLEAVER. No.

MARKHAM. So you know of no one who might have been in Miss O'Dell's confidence.

CLEAVER. If it's a question of someone who had her confidence, I might suggest Lucinda Lindquist. She was pretty close to the Canary at one time – if you take my meaning.

MARKHAM. Really!

CLEAVER. She's just the sort of woman the Canary might have selected as a source of income. And I know this, she came to see the Canary a good deal more than a woman of her standing should.

MARKHAM. You've no one else in mind who might know something helpful?

CLEAVER. No, no one.

MARKHAM. Thank you, anyway.

CLEAVER. I happened to notice Lucinda Lindquist here this evening.

MARKHAM. In that case, do ask her to join us.

CHARLES CLEAVER EXITS. ENTER LUCINDA LINDQUIST

MARKHAM. Ah, Miss Lindquist I would like to speak to you about Canary O'Dell.

LINDQUIST. Ah, yes. Canary! A most unfortunate and tragic affair! In just what way can I be of service to you?

MARKHAM. I understand you and the Canary were close –

LINDQUIST. So what if we were?

MARKHAM. You realise that it is the duty of every citizen to assist the authorities in bringing a murderer to justice. And if there is anything you can tell me which will help towards that end, I shall certainly expect you to say.

LINDQUIST. I shall, of course, do all I can to assist you.

MARKHAM. There's no need to beat about the bush. I suspect that Miss Canary may have told you certain personal things which may have direct bearing on her death.

LINDQUIST. I will confess I came to regard Canary with a certain - shall I say, sisterly liking? But I doubt if she was even aware of this mild sentiment on my part.

MARKHAM. And she never at any time told you of any private or personal affairs that were causing her anxiety?

LINDQUIST. No. I know, in a general way, her manner of living.

MARKHAM. Oh?

LINDQUIST. She suffered from her nerves. A consequence of too many late hours, irregular and rich eating! She was a modern woman in a modern age.

MARKHAM. When did you see her last?

LINDQUIST. A fortnight ago, perhaps! Though it may have been longer! I really can't recall.

MARKHAM. Did the meeting take place here?

LINDQUIST. It did, yes.

MARKHAM. You called on her a great deal, I believe.

LINDQUIST. Is it the function of the police to harass respectable people with insulting questions?

MARKHAM. Would you be good enough to tell me where you were today between two and three?

LINDQUIST. My whereabouts today is of no concern of yours. What do you mean by these contemptible insinuations?

MARKHAM. Please answer the question.

LINDQUIST. I went to see an aged aunt. But she wasn't in so I came away. I left her a note to say that I called.

MARKHAM. How convenient.

LINDQUIST. I resent that implication -

MARKHAM. I do apologise. But you must understand, a young woman has been murdered. But for now, you may go. And thank you for your help. I take it you won't leave here until our investigation has been completed?

LINDQUIST. I have no intention of going anywhere.

MARKHAM. Oh, as you leave, could you ask the officer outside to call in Sarah Spotswoode to see me?

LUCINDA LINDQUIST EXITS. ENTER SARAH SPOTSWOODE

MARKHAM. It's only fair to tell you, I may have to call you as a witness.

SPOTSWOODE. I see your point. But it would be terrible for me if my delinquencies became known. I'm in an unpleasant position, and naturally feel quite sensitive about all this.

MARKHAM. That may be avoided. I promise you that you will not be called upon unless it is necessary. And now what I especially wanted to ask you is this. Do you happen to know a Lucinda Lindquist?

SPOTSWOODE. I am acquainted with her.

MARKHAM. And did you ever hear her mention the name of Tony Skeel?

SPOTSWOODE. Never.

MARKHAM. Do you happen to remember anything unusual occurring today during the half hour you remained with Miss Canary after lunch?

SPOTSWOODE. On the contrary! We chatted a while, she seemed tired, I came away.

MARKHAM. And you came back again to collect your phone.

SPOTSWOODE. Yes, Then I called a taxi.

MARKHAM. And yet, it now seems that some other person was hiding in the room when you were there. And Miss Canary's screams would indicate that the other person came from hiding a few minutes after you went. Did you not have any suspicion of the fact when you heard her call for help?

SPOTSWOODE. I did at first, naturally. But when she assured me that nothing was the matter, and told me to go home, I attributed her screams to a bad dream. I knew she had been tired so I naturally concluded she had dozed off and called out in her sleep.

MARKHAM. It's a harrowing situation.

SPOTSWOODE. I don't suppose you'd let me into her room to look for one or two trinkets I gave the Canary. CD's, that sort of thing!

MARKHAM. I see.

SPOTSWOODE. Sentimental value, you understand. She meant a lot to me. I cared a good deal for the girl.

MARKHAM. I'm afraid that's not possible.

SPOTSWOODE. I understand.

MARKHAM. Thank you for your help.

SPOTSWOODE EXITS

MARKHAM. What did you make of those three interviews?

O'DELL. I may be evil-minded, but Charles Cleaver didn't impress me as a pillar of truth.

MARKHAM. It isn't exactly pleasant to admit having been taken in and blackmailed by a charmer.

O'DELL. Still, if he got his letters back in June, why did he continue paying court to my sister?

MARKHAM. At any rate, he gave us Lucinda Lindquist, a possible source of further information.

O'DELL. Funny how an empty-headed type like my sister could attract a woman of Lucinda's standing. I have to admit, what I'm learning about the Canary of the clan is opening my eyes somewhat.

MARKHAM. Aren't you upset by all these revelations?

O'DELL. I'm too intrigued to be upset. All this is like a murder mystery -

MARKHAM. Which of course it is!

O'DELL. My sister's always led a colourful life. As you may know, she spent a number of years trying to break into the acting profession. The most she ever got was a couple of radio plays.

MARKHAM. So, who's next on our list of likely suspects?

O'DELL. Lewis Mannix.

MARKHAM. It's funny how all the key players to this dreadful state of affairs are all here this evening.

O'DELL. At least it makes life easy. Clearly the circle of friends around my sister was a close one.

MARKHAM. Have Mr. Mannix come and join us.

ENTER LEWIS MANNIX

MARKHAM. Mr Mannix. As you know, Canary O'Dell was murdered earlier today and in the course of our enquiries we learn that you knew her quite well.

MANNIX. Sure, I knew the Canary - a long time ago. A lovely girl! Too bad she didn't go on with show business. But I haven't seen her for over a year - not to speak to.

MARKHAM. You had a quarrel with her perhaps?

MANNIX. Well, now, I wouldn't go so far as to say we quarrelled. You might say we disagreed - got tired of the arrangement and decided to separate, kind of drifted apart. Last thing I told her was, if she ever needed a friend she'd know where to find me.

MARKHAM. Did she ever make an attempt to blackmail you?

MANNIX. Certainly not! What gave you such an idea?

MARKHAM. She may have been extorting money from one or two of her admirers.

MANNIX. Well, well! You don't say! Maybe it was Charles Cleaver she blackmailed.

MARKHAM. Why do you say Cleaver?

MANNIX. No reason. Just thought it might be him. Like I told you, he knew the Canary.

MARKHAM. What do you know about Miss Canary's relations with a Lucinda Lindquist?

MANNIX. Nothing.

MARKHAM. Who else besides Cleaver did she know well?

MANNIX. I really couldn't say.

MARKHAM. Ever heard of Tony Skeel?

MANNIX. What makes you think I heard of this Skeel fellow?

MARKHAM. Can you think of no one who might have borne Miss Canary a grudge?

MANNIX. Not at all.

MARKHAM. Thank you for your time. Mr. Mannix.

LEWIS MANNIX EXITS

MARKHAM. I give up. This case is bafflement itself.

O'DELL. Not if we accept that this was not the crime of a professional thief but the wilful act of a clever killer who doubtless spent weeks in the preparation.

MARKHAM. That's as maybe. What we need now is evidence, not theories. Which brings us back to Tony Skeel!

O'DELL. Skeel - ah, yes. Skeel ripped the jewel box open all right - but it's the only thing he did do. It's the only thing that was left for him to do. Because I think there were two people involved in this case.

MARKHAM. What makes you think that?

O'DELL. The knife! That amateurish assault upon the jewel box with a knife couldn't have been made *after* the box had been prised open - it would have had to be made *before*. The murderer didn't care if he got the box open or not. He merely wanted it to look as if he had *tried* to get it open. So he used the knife and left it lying around.

MARKHAM. So when was Tony Skeel in your sister's room?

O'DELL. He was either in the room when the bogus robbery was being staged or else had come upon the scene when it was over and the real villain had cleared out.

MARKHAM. So, who did kill your sister?

O'DELL. I haven't the slightest idea. But if you are to find the murderer you must look for a shrewd killer with nerves of steel who was in danger of being ruined by my sister.

MARKHAM. There are only four people who could have any remote reason for murdering your sister. Lewis Mannix, Lucinda Lindquist, Charles Cleaver and Sarah Spotswoode!

O'DELL. It appears then that we have enough to draw on. What more do you want?

MARKHAM. Lewis Mannix was through with your sister over a year ago. Charles Cleaver and Sarah Spotswoode have watertight alibis and that leaves Lucinda Lindquist -

O'DELL. Of course, she's also got an alibi of sorts, and it may be a genuine one. Therefore out of four possibilities, not one of them is promising.

MARKHAM. In that case, the crime is impossible to solve.

THEY EXIT

THREE

ENTER MARKHAM AND THE SERGEANT

MARKHAM. Sergeant, find Tony Skeel.

ENTER TONY SKEEL

SKEEL. I'm Tony Skeel. What do you want?

MARKHAM. I understand you were trying to sell this ring during dinner. *(Markham shows Skeel a ring)*

SKEEL. So, what of it?

MARKHAM. Does the ring belong to Miss Canary O'Dell?

SKEEL. Maybe.

MARKHAM. I put it to you that Miss Canary was wearing this ring when she died.

SKEEL. I'm not saying anything.

MARKHAM. You don't have to. This ring connects you to the murder of Canary O'Dell and the robbery.

SKEEL. Canary gave me the ring a week ago. I admit I saw her this morning, but when I returned to the hotel about twelve o'clock she was out. I then went away.

MARKHAM. There's also the question of the fingerprints.

SKEEL. That's not evidence. I could have made them when I saw the Canary this morning. What you need for a murder is more than circumstantial evidence, Inspector. A good criminal lawyer will have me discharged in twenty minutes.

MARKHAM. That'll do for now, Skeel. Just don't leave town.

SKEEL. There is someone you might want to talk to.

MARKHAM. Oh, and who might that be?

SKEEL. Alys La Fosse! She's an old friend of Canary's. And before you ask, she's here this evening. Now, you must excuse me. I need some air.

MARKHAM. By all means! My Sergeant will accompany you.

TONY SKEEL EXITS WITH THE SERGEANT. ENTER ALYS LA FOSSE

MARKHAM. Ah, Miss La Fosse –

ALYS. I don't know nuffink and I've got nuffink to say.

MARKHAM. What do you know of a man name of Tony Skeel?

ALYS. That cheap crook? He hasn't the nerve to strangle a cat.

MARKHAM. Who said he did?

ALYS. Why else would you be talking about him?

MARKHAM. Perhaps you could help us in our enquiries.

ALYS. I was told to keep out of this.

MARKHAM. Who told you to keep out of it?

ALYS. A friend, if you must know. He's very well known around here and there might be a scandal -

MARKHAM. Who is this man?

ALYS. If you must know, he's Lewis Mannix. Lewis used to go around with the Canary. That's why he didn't want me to get mixed up in this affair. He said the police would bother him with questions and his name would get in the papers.

MARKHAM. Do you happen to know where Mr. Mannix was this afternoon?

ALYS. Of course I know! He was here with me all day.

MARKHAM. Tell me, Alys, what do you know about a Charles Cleaver? I understand he was a friend of Miss Canary's.

ALYS. Oh, Charlies okay. He was certainly soft on the Canary. Even when she chucked him for that Spotswoode woman! He still chased after her, sent her flowers, that sort of thing. Some men are like that.

MARKHAM. One more question. What was the situation between Miss Canary and Lucinda Lindquist?

ALYS. Lucinda was wildly in love with Canary. And Canary led the poor woman on. But she was sorry for it afterwards.

MARKHAM. Why?

ALYS. Because Lucinda got jealous! She used to pester the life out of Canary. And once, she threatened to shoot Canary and then shoot herself. I told Canary to look out for her. But she didn't seem to be afraid.

MARKHAM. And there wasn't anyone else who felt the same way? Anyone Miss Canary had reason to fear?

ALYS. Canary didn't know many people intimately.

MARKHAM. Thank you for all your help.

ALYS. Who do you think killed Canary? Lewis says it was probably a burglar who wanted her jewels.

O'DELL. *(Interrupting)* Tell me, Alys, why are you lying to us?

ALYS. I beg your pardon!

O'DELL. Lewis Mannix wasn't with you all day today. I can see it in your face. You can pull the wool over Inspector Markham's eyes -

ALYS. I'm not going to say any more. If I say Lewis was with me all day, then that's what I'm saying. And nobody can prove any different.

O'DELL. I hope he's worth protecting.

ALYS. What's that supposed to mean?

O'DELL. If he wasn't with you, then he was with somebody else. Think about it.

ALYS. I don't have to think about anything. Now, if that is all –

SHE EXITS

MARKHAM. How did you know she was lying?

O'DELL. I didn't. As you know, women can be so shrewd, yet so gullible. Most women can read most men with remarkable accuracy - except when it comes to their own men. Lewis Mannix most probably told her he was working or something. Naturally, she's suspicious but can't bring herself to believe that he's mixed up with my sister's murder. So she lies, protects him.

MARKHAM. Have you ever thought of joining the police force?

O'DELL. Unfortunately we can't get away from the fact that Charles Cleaver's alibi has him being booked for speeding on the motorway.

MARKHAM. If he wasn't on the motorway then who was?

O'DELL. That's for him to know and you to find out.

MARKHAM. *(Realising)* Of course, he's got a brother. A simple enough ruse! I think we should talk to him again.

O'DELL. Before we do that, we need another chat with Sarah Spotswoode.

MARKHAM. The trouble is, we don't have any real evidence against anybody.

O'DELL. Certain parts of the puzzle are missing. Find them and everything will fit like a beautiful mosaic.

MARKHAM. What's needed is some process to enable us to clear up some of the human flotsam that's cluttering up the case.

O'DELL. Let's speak to Mr. Mannix.

ENTER LEWIS MANNIX

MARKHAM. I'm not at all satisfied with what you told me earlier, Mr. Mannix.

MANNIX. If I knew anything about Canary's death, I would say.

MARKHAM. I'm delighted to hear it. First, please tell me where you were today between two and three.

MANNIX. Why should I tell you that? Am I suspected of murdering the Canary?

MARKHAM. An unwillingness to answer my question certainly puts you under suspicion.

MANNIX. I've got nothing to hide.

MARKHAM. Why are you so uneasy, Mr. Mannix?

MANNIX. Me, uneasy? I'm just wondering what my private life has to do with all this.

MARKHAM. I'll tell you. Miss Canary was murdered between two and three. No one came or went through the front door and the side door was bolted.

MANNIX. Assuming the side door was bolted.

MARKHAM. Go on.

MANNIX. That side door wasn't bolted this afternoon. And I know who sneaked out of it at ten to three.

MARKHAM. I think you'd better tell us the whole story.

MANNIX. Oh, I'm going to tell it all right. You're on the right track in one respect - I wasn't where I was supposed to be. I was here in this hotel. I spent the afternoon with a friend. There's no harm in that, is there?

MARKHAM. What time did you arrive?

MANNIX. I don't know, around lunchtime.

MARKHAM. And you entered the hotel through the front door?

MANNIX. No, I entered through the side door. My lady friend unbolted the door for me. It's nobody's business who I see and I like to keep it that way.

MARKHAM. And did you spend the whole afternoon with this lady friend?

MANNIX. What do you think?

MARKHAM. So what happened at ten to three?

MANNIX. I was about to leave and just as I opened the door of her room I saw someone sneaking away from the Canary's door.

MARKHAM. Who was it?

MANNIX. Charles Cleaver!

MARKHAM. What did you do then?

MANNIX. Nothing! I didn't think much about it. I knew Cleaver was after the Canary, I just assumed he'd been to see her. Naturally, I didn't want Cleaver to see me. I just waited for him to leave.

MARKHAM. By the side door?

MANNIX. Yes. I went out the same way.

MARKHAM. Why didn't you tell us this earlier?

MANNIX. I didn't want to get involved.

MARKHAM. Did you see anyone else in the hall?

MANNIX. No.

MARKHAM. Did you hear anything from Miss Canary's room?

MANNIX. No.

MARKHAM. And you're certain of the time Cleaver left?

MANNIX. Certain!

MARKHAM. Thank you. You can give my sergeant the name of your lady friend – he could do with a bit of excitement.

LEWIS MANNIX EXITS

O'DELL. What do you think to all that?

MARKHAM. We've found one missing piece of the puzzle. But I'm still laying money on Tony Skeel. I know a professional job when I see it. And as for evidence, we still have the fingerprints and the ring. I admit, Lucinda Lindquist and Charles Cleaver don't exactly inspire one with confidence but one can't get away from the fact that it's Tony Skeel who's got a visible motive and he's the only one we have any evidence on.

O'DELL. Fingerprints and rings don't make him a killer. No, my money's on Lewis Mannix. I just don't like him, which I suppose is hardly grounds for conviction.

MARKHAM. There's too many loose ends for comfort.

O'DELL. There were definitely two people in on this act. Two strangers acting separately! One a professional burglar, the other a desperate murderer! Evidence the document case. It was empty. Now, what's bothering me is that the case wasn't forced open, it was unlocked with a key, a key taken from my sister perhaps. Also, a case like that wouldn't contain valuables. most likely it contained letters and documents - far more valuable than any jewel. If Tony Skeel is our professional burglar, then he didn't open the document case - had no reason to! No, somebody else opened the case.

MARKHAM. Go on.

O'DELL. Take Charles Cleaver, for instance. He admitted that he paid my sister a lot of money last June to get back his letters. But suppose he never paid the money. Suppose he came here today to take the letters. And if Cleaver did take the letters and if one of those letters was dated later than last June, then we have proof positive -

MARKHAM. Assuming he's kept the letters.

O'DELL. I think we should speak to Mr. Cleaver.

MARKHAM. Will you go and fetch him?

O'DELL. With pleasure! I wouldn't miss the expression on his face for the world.

MARKHAM. An expression hardly constitutes guilt.

ENTER CHARLES CLEAVER

MARKHAM. Mr. Cleaver. I need to talk to you again. Why did you tell me you were on the motorway earlier today?

CLEAVER. I wanted an alibi. My brother, who had borrowed the car, gave me a ready-made alibi. He was driving my car on the motorway and had all my I. D.

MARKHAM. Why did you need an alibi?

CLEAVER. I didn't need it. People knew I'd been seeing the Canary and people also knew she was blackmailing me.

MARKHAM. Is that your only reason for concocting this alibi?

CLEAVER. Isn't that reason enough? I just didn't want to be involved.

MARKHAM. You were seen coming out of Miss Canary's room at 2.50 today. Between 2.40 and three o'clock, Miss Canary was strangled and robbed. What do you say to that?

CLEAVER. There's not much to say really. I went to see the Canary, but I didn't enter her room, I didn't even knock on the door. Something made me stop.

MARKHAM. Just a moment, how did you enter the hotel?

CLEAVER. By the side door! Canary opens it for me. She doesn't want people to know her business.

MARKHAM. Okay, then what?

CLEAVER. I listened at her door for a minute. I thought there might have been someone else with her. I didn't want to knock in case she had company.

MARKHAM. Why did you think there was someone else there? Was it because you phoned her earlier and the phone was answered by some other person?

CLEAVER. There's no point in denying it.

MARKHAM. What did this person say to you when you phoned?

CLEAVER. When I asked for the Canary, I was told she wasn't in and they hung up.

MARKHAM. So, you listened at her door. What stopped you from knocking on the door?

CLEAVER. I heard a man's voice inside.

MARKHAM. Could you identify the voice?

CLEAVER. It wasn't very clear. I think it was the same one that answered the phone.

MARKHAM. Could you make out what was being said?

CLEAVER. It sounded like he was saying, *"Oh, my God!"* Over and over again! And it wasn't in ecstasy, either.

MARKHAM. When you heard this man's voice, what did you do?

CLEAVER. I left the hotel.

MARKHAM. Tell me, what were you doing between the time you rang Miss Canary and the moment you entered the hotel?

CLEAVER. I was upset. I knew the Canary was seeing someone else. I went for a walk.

MARKHAM. Is that when you met Lucinda Lindquist?

CLEAVER. I arrived at the hotel a little before 2.30. I ran into Lucinda Lindquist, she was standing outside. She spoke to me. She told me someone was with Canary in her room. I then walked around a corner and phoned Canary. As I said, a man answered. Then I walked back to the hotel. The rest you know.

MARKHAM. You told me it was last June that you bought your letters back from Miss Canary. Do you recall the date?

CLEAVER. Not exactly!

MARKHAM. So if we search your home and find the letters, we'll find that the dates correspond to your story.

CLEAVER. Very well! The fact is, I didn't pay my blackmail to the Canary until three weeks ago. I told you it was June in order to set back the date as far as possible. The older the affair, the less chance of being implicated!

MARKHAM. That will do for now.

CLEAVER. I've got nothing to do with this, you know.

MARKHAM. Then you have nothing to fear. Lucinda Lindquist is here. Ask her to join us.

CHARLES CLEAVER EXITS. ENTER LUCINDA LINDQUIST

MARKHAM. Ah, Miss Lindquist. We understand that your interest in Miss Canary was a bit more than sisterly. In fact, you were jealous of her.

LINDQUIST. Jealousy does not necessarily go with infatuation. Not that my emotions are any of your business.

MARKHAM. When your emotions get the better of you and you end up threatening Miss Canary's life, then they become my business. And given the fact that Miss Canary has since been murdered, the law is naturally curious.

LINDQUIST. Threats rarely turn to action. They are empty, that's the whole point of them. Canary was in the habit of playing loose with my emotions. She knew how I felt and chose to exploit it. She was a very perverse young woman.

MARKHAM. Leaving that to one side, I would like to know where you were this afternoon between two and three. And please, the truth this time.

LINDQUIST. The fact is, I was at home. Then I arrived at the hotel about two o'clock. I stood outside for half an hour and then left.

MARKHAM. I think you'd better elaborate. Start from the beginning.

LINDQUIST. I knew Canary was going to lunch with Spotswoode, and the thought of it began to pray on my mind. As I sat at home, I felt myself becoming insanely jealous. You see, I had already threatened to kill Canary and myself and now that threat was becoming more and more attractive - and inevitable.

MARKHAM. What happened then?

LINDQUIST. I put a gun in my handbag and left my home. I thought Canary and Spotswoode would be returning from lunch soon and I intended to force my way into her room and shoot all three of us. From across the street, I saw them enter the hotel, it was about two o'clock. But then I came face to face with the awful reality of it all. I hesitated.

MARKHAM. And?

LINDQUIST. For half an hour I waited. Then, as I was about to enter the hotel, Charles Cleaver came along. He stopped and spoke. I thought he was calling on Canary, so I told him she already had a visitor. He then walked away. Then Spotswoode came out of the hotel and jumped into a taxi and left. My plan had been thwarted - I had waited too long.

MARKHAM. Lucky for you, your story hangs together with our other evidence. Please wait. We may need you further.

LUCINDA LINDQUIST EXITS

MARKHAM. So, we have everyone at the scene of the crime.

O'DELL. But nobody saw Tony Skeel. All we have to do now is find out who was with Skeel in my sister's room today.

MARKHAM. It boils down to Lewis Mannix, Charles Cleaver and Lucinda Lindquist. And if we accept Cleaver's story, each of them had an opportunity of getting into your sister's room between two and three o'clock.

O'DELL. But we only have Cleaver's word that Lucinda Lindquist was in the area.

MARKHAM. What a mess. And the cry! *"Oh, my God!"* might have been made by either Mannix or Lucinda - provided Cleaver really heard it.

O'DELL. He heard it all right. Cleaver's not that clever.

MARKHAM. But if Cleaver heard the voice, then it must eliminate him as a suspect.

O'DELL. Not at all! He may have heard it after leaving my sister's room and realised, for the first time that someone had been hiding in the wardrobe. It might have been a horrified Skeel who emerged from his hiding place to witness the sight of my sister strangled.

MARKHAM. Okay. Someone besides Skeel got into your sister's room and then Skeel hid in the wardrobe. But, that being the case, the actual murderer didn't see Skeel -

O'DELL. Ah, but the question is, did Skeel see the murderer?

MARKHAM. I think it is time for us to speak to Mr. Skeel again.

O'DELL. Perhaps we've been looking at him from the wrong angle. Up until now he's been a prime suspect - perhaps he's more of a material witness.

MARKHAM. We do have a further problem. *(Looking at the audience)* All these people here!

O'DELL. They'll all leave eventually.

MARKHAM. They can't.

O'DELL. Why can't they?

MARKHAM. For one thing, our suspects are among their number. If they go, our suspects go. And for another thing, I can't see them leaving without having their curiosity satisfied.

O'DELL. What, they won't go until we discover who the murderer is? I'll tell you what, why not get them to write down the name of the murderer and a possible motive and we'll consider the evidence.

MARKHAM. Worth a try, I suppose. I'm just thankful we only have the one murder to solve.

ENTER TONY SKEEL. HE HAS BEEN STABBED. HE COLLAPSES

MARKHAM. What on earth!

O'DELL. He's been stabbed. Who is it?

MARKHAM. You won't believe this. It's Tony Skeel.

O'DELL. We must get him out.

MARKHAM. I'll go and phone for an ambulance.

THEY EXIT WITH TONY SKEEL

FOUR

ENTER MARKHAM AND O'DELL

MARKHAM. Ladies and gentlemen, can I have your attention. As you know, Tony Skeel has been killed. You might like to know that he was stabbed with his own chisel, the same chisel which was used to prise open the jewel box. *(Markham lays out the chisel)* You might also like to know, that he was carrying Canary O'Dell's jewels.

O'DELL. It looks like Skeel knew who killed my sister and the murderer also knew that Skeel knew. Which makes him innocent of murder! Not that it will do him much good now. Pretty soon the fog will lift, the sun will shine, the birds will sing.

MARKHAM. *(Looking at the audience)* You realise we still have people out there. They must be getting impatient. I'll tell you what, let's play some music. That'll keep them going. Is there a stereo here?

O'DELL. Not really. My sister had one in her room. It was mine originally. I took the liberty of retrieving it before it got nicked. Your nice sergeant said it was okay.

MARKHAM. *(Looks at the stereo)* There's a CD already in the deck. I'll just see what it is.

O'DELL. Never mind all that for now.

MARKHAM. Right! What we need is answers to the following questions. How did your sister's murderer get into her room? Why did they kill her? And who did the dreadful deed?

O'DELL. And those questions have to apply to Tony Skeel as well as the murderer.

MARKHAM. All right! Let's deal with Skeel first.

O'DELL. Skeel needed money and after his unsuccessful attempt to extort it from my sister last week, he came here today. He knocked on her door, slipped down the hall, and unbolted the side door before returning to my sister's room. He then knocked again for effect - no answer. After a suitable pause, he returned to the hall and then left the hotel only to return to the scene of the crime by the side door.

MARKHAM. So far, so good!

O'DELL. When my sister returned with Spotswoode, Skeel quickly hid in the wardrobe and stayed there until Spotswoode departed. Skeel then revealed himself to my sister and a row broke out about money. In the middle of their tiff, the phone rang and Skeel snatched it up saying that my sister was out. The tiff was resumed. But soon Spotswoode returned to collect her phone. Skeel once again hid in the wardrobe. After Spotswoode left for the second time, Skeel and Canary continued their row only to be interrupted again – this time by the killer.

MARKHAM. Skeel then hid in the wardrobe again. Of course, being curious, Skeel peeped through the keyhole to see who the other person was.

O'DELL. So you can imagine his horror when the second person suddenly seized my sister by the throat and throttled her. Skeel must have been petrified.

MARKHAM. What did the murderer do next?

O'DELL. We'll never know for sure, now that Skeel's dead. But I daresay he, or she, opened the document case and pocketed a number of incriminating letters. Then, the fireworks began. My sister's killer proceeded to wreck the room and everything in it. The murderer then stripped the jewellery off my sister's hands to give the impression of a professional burglary. And all the while, Skeel remained hidden, scared witless.

MARKHAM. Hidden in the wardrobe!

O'DELL. In time, the murderer left and it was safe for Skeel to come out of hiding. Imagine the poor man, weak-kneed and in a cold sweat. My sister lay strangled, the room a tip. Skeel then realised his own position. He was alone with a murdered woman. He was known to have been intimate with my sister and he was a professional burglar to boot. Nobody would believe a word he said. He had to get away.

MARKHAM. Before leaving, he chiselled open the jewel box, which the murderer could only dent with a knife, and took the ring which he later tried to sell. He then wiped away his fingerprints, forgetting the inside of the wardrobe. A crook, no matter how clever, always overlooks something.

O'DELL. Skeel either knew or recognised the murderer and, once free, felt able to blackmail the real culprit. And furthermore, my theory does fit in with all the evidence.

MARKHAM. So, who is the murderer?

O'DELL. Perhaps your Sergeant should collect the suspect sheets. They may provide us with some valuable information.

MARKHAM. Sergeant, would you mind.

THE SERGEANT COLLECTS THE SHEETS

MARKHAM. We have four possibilities. Lewis Mannix, Charles Cleaver, Lucinda Lindquist and Sarah Spotswoode! Now, no one actually saw your sister alive after Spotswoode left the place.

O'DELL. But my sister spoke to Sarah Spotswoode through the door. Bill Jessup heard her. Unless it was Skeel disguising his voice!

MARKHAM. Good heavens, no! Skeel didn't want anyone to know he was there.

O'DELL. So, how did the murderer do it?

MARKHAM. The only surety we have relates to Spotswoode.

O'DELL. Correct. She couldn't have been in two places at the same time.

MARKHAM. I need to think this one through. Look, let's play some music. We could do with some inspiration while we study the sheets. *(Markham plays the CD)*

CD. *Nothing is the matter! I'm sorry! Everything is all right! Please go home! And don't worry!*

MARKHAM. Well, well, well! Perhaps this is the break we've been looking for.

O'DELL. I have it! Our friend Spotswoode <u>did</u> have the means to be in two places at the same time after all. Now it all fits into place. After she killed my sister, she put on the CD and left. While she waited for her taxi, the CD reached the right point and Spotswoode was able to synchronise her dialogue to fit in with the pauses on the CD. It also explains her eagerness to gain access to my sister's room. She said she wanted the CD for sentimental reasons - nobody would have given it another thought.

MARKHAM. How on earth did she get hold of your sister on CD?

O'DELL. My sister was an actress. She'd done radio plays. Spotswoode probably edited stuff from her plays.

MARKHAM. What about Skeel?

O'DELL. As we guessed, he would have witnessed my sister's murder and clambered out of the wardrobe when the coast was clear. Imagine his horror when the CD played - and his greater horror when Spotswoode spoke through the door. This must have puzzled Skeel. But I daresay the significance of it all soon dawned on him. He knew who the murderer was and saw a golden opportunity for blackmail.

MARKHAM. But what of Cleaver's phone call?

O'DELL. Skeel answered the phone and merely said my sister was out.

MARKHAM. But why didn't he take the CD with him?

O'DELL. Bad move. The evidence had to remain in the room. If Skeel had the CD all Spotswoode had to do was accuse Skeel of mischief. No, Skeel had to leave the CD in my sister's room and sting Spotswoode immediately.

MARKHAM. That's amazing.

O'DELL. My sister had to die so Spotswoode arranged it all down to the finest detail. She took every precaution possible, aiming to return to the scene of the crime to collect the CD. But fate moved against her. Not being able to return was a blow. Our interest in music hasn't helped and Skeel hiding away in a wardrobe was downright contrary.

MARKHAM. How can you be so calm about all this?

O'DELL. Don't forget, my sister was also a blackmailer.

MARKHAM. I think we should speak to Spotswoode. It's always the person one least expects. *(To the Sergeant)* Sergeant, fetch Sarah Spotswoode.

THE SERGEANT BRINGS ON SARAH SPOTSWOODE

MARKHAM. Sarah Spotswoode, I'm arresting you for the murder of Canary O'Dell. Do you recognise this?

(Markham plays the CD again) "Nothing is the matter! I'm sorry! Everything is all right! Please go home! And don't worry!"

SPOTSWOODE. I had no alternative. It was a gamble but had I not taken action, I would have lost terribly.

MARKHAM. Killing someone is rather drastic, don't you think?

SPOTSWOODE. Canary demanded the impossible of me. Not content with bleeding me financially, she demanded I should leave my job and live with her. I love my job. Can you imagine the scandal? So when I refused her demands, she threatened to expose our relationship to all and sundry. Canary was in a position to ruin me.

MARKHAM. You're obviously not a woman of half -way measures. You clearly have little talent for compromise. And what of Skeel?

SPOTSWOODE. What of him? He tried to blackmail me.

MARKHAM. And what of the jewellery?

SPOTSWOODE. I took it to give the impression of a common burglary. It's ironic, I most probably paid for most of it myself. But I couldn't keep it. I would have given it to Skeel, but it wasn't enough.

MARKHAM. And what of Miss O'Dell?

SPOTSWOODE. What of her? She may have been a Canary, but she picked my bones like a vulture.

MARKHAM. There is one thing I don't understand. If you meant to kill her, why did you leave her room, only to return for your phone?

SPOTSWOODE. I needed to strengthen my alibi. I wanted as many people as possible to see me come and go. I originally intended to shoot the Canary.

MARKHAM. *(To the Sergeant)* Sergeant, take her outside.

SPOTSWOODE. Don't worry, I won't try to escape. I know when the game's up.

SERGEANT EXITS WITH SPOTSWOODE

MARKHAM. There's one thing that puzzles still.

O'DELL. What's that?

MARKHAM. The occasional *"Oh, my God!"* from your sister's room.

O'DELL. Tony Skeel was caught in a trap. He must have paced up and down for ages thinking of a plan. I daresay he called to the Deity with an occasional plea.

A SHOT RINGS OUT. ENTER SARAH SPOTSWOODE COVERED IN BLOOD. SHE HAS A GUN IN HER HAND

MARKHAM. What on earth –

O'DELL. It's Spotswoode. She's shot herself.

MARKHAM. Quick. We must call another ambulance. We've had enough deaths around here for one night.

THEY EXIT

END OF PLAY

An English Murder

The Phœnix

A death occurs,
then another,
then another.
Is it murder ?
Who is the killer?

AN ENGLISH MURDER

Warbeck Hall. Winter 1951. Guests gather for Christmas. There is a raging snow storm outside and the house is cut off from the outside world. A death occurs, then another, then another. Is it murder? If so, who is the killer?

Can Sergeant Rogers from Special Branch stop the bloodshed around him? Can the absent-minded Doctor Bottwink assist? Can the audience guess the identity of the killer?

An English Murder is based on a classic novel by Cyril Hare.

Characters
Doctor Bottwink
Sergeant Rogers
Briggs the Butler
Robert Warbeck
Lady Camilla
Mrs Carstairs
Sir Julius
Susan Briggs
Lord Warbeck

Murder Mysteries Vol 2

ONE

WARBECK HALL. CHRISTMAS EVE, 1951

ENTER DR BOTTWINK AND BRIGGS THE BUTLER

BOTTWINK. Ah, Briggs, there you are. Do you think I could have some tea? If it's no trouble.

BRIGGS. It's no trouble at all, Dr Bottwink. I generally have a cup myself about this time.

BOTTWINK. None the less, it is kind of you, Briggs. Tea is very comforting. It warms the cockles.

BRIGGS. Just so. It is very cold. Snow is already falling. We can expect a white Christmas. It is nearly midnight -

BOTTWINK. Nearly midnight! Is it as late as that? One loses all account of time in a place like this. Is tomorrow really to be Christmas Day?

BRIGGS. Tomorrow is Christmas Day, sir. You must take my word for it.

BOTTWINK. I had no idea. I have been so much longer on my research than I intended. I have trespassed on Lord Warbeck's hospitality long enough as it is.

BRIGGS. I took the liberty of raising the subject with his lordship just now when I brought him his tea, and he expressed the desire that if it met with your convenience, you should remain as his guest over the festive season – and seeing that it is now too late for you to return to the village -

BOTTWINK. That is very kind of him. I shall take the opportunity of thanking him personally, if he is able to see me. How is he tonight, by the way?

BRIGGS. His lordship is better, thank you. He is up, but not yet down.

BOTTWINK. Up, but not yet down. Up, but not yet down. English is such a beautiful language.

BRIGGS. Quite.

BOTTWINK. By the way, Briggs, you spoke just now of the festive season. I imagine that in present circumstances the festivities will be of a purely notional character?

BRIGGS. I beg your pardon?

BOTTWINK. I mean, there will, in fact, be no junketing – what with Lord Warbeck being so ill.

BRIGGS. I am unable to say precisely what form the celebrations will take. But I think it may be assumed that Christmas will be quiet. His lordship has only invited a few members of his family.

BOTTWINK. Oh, there are to be guests, then? Who, for example?

BRIGGS. Sir Julius Warbeck arrived this evening.

BOTTWINK. Sir Julius is the Chancellor of the Exchequer in the present Labour government, is he not?

BRIGGS. Precisely. He has arrived with a member of Special Branch – a Sergeant Rogers.

BOTTWINK. I thought Lord Warbeck's political views were of a very different character.

BRIGGS. Sir Julius is coming here simply in his capacity as Lord Warbeck's first cousin.

BOTTWINK. I shall be delighted to meet Sir Julius. Perhaps you can tell me who else I am to meet?

BRIGGS. There are just two ladies. Lady Camilla Prendergast and Mrs Carstairs. Lady Camilla is not directly related to the family but is still treated as such. As for Mrs Carstairs, her father was rector of this parish for many years and she was brought up in the house, so to speak. That is all the party – except for Mr Robert, of course.

BOTTWINK. Robert Warbeck, the son of the house? He is to be here for Christmas?

BRIGGS. Naturally.

BOTTWINK. I suppose it is natural. Curious that I should not have thought of him. Briggs, I suppose it would be impossible for me to have my meals in the servants' hall? I don't think I shall enjoy sitting down at table with Robert Warbeck. You do know who Mr Robert is, don't you?

BRIGGS. Of course I do. He is his lordship's son and heir.

BOTTWINK. He is also the president of the League of Liberty, a Fascist organisation.

BRIGGS. Is that so? I have never been greatly interested in politics.

BOTTWINK. Thank you, Briggs. I must say, I am not looking forward to meeting Robert Warbeck.

BRIGGS EXITS. ENTER ROBERT WARBECK

ROBERT. Ah, Briggs told me you were working here on my father's papers. I hope you are not too cold. I am Robert Warbeck.

BOTTWINK. *(Coldly)* One does not easily perish merely of cold, so long as food is available.

ROBERT. I am afraid it is difficult nowadays to make guests as comfortable as we should wish.

BOTTWINK. Indeed, Mr Robert, I assure you, it is nothing. I should not have spoken as I did, even as a joke. I have been many times much colder, and I repeat, it is nothing.

ROBERT. No doubt you have found it colder in your own country. *(Sneering)* What is your country, may I ask?

BOTTWINK. That would be a little difficult to say exactly. By nationality I have been Austrian and Czech and German – in that order. But I am a bit Russian also, and, as it happens, I was born in Hungary. So there are a good many ingredients in my make-up.

ROBERT. A mixed bag, then?

BOTTWINK. Of course. I wonder whether, in all the circumstances, it might perhaps be preferable if I did not accept your father's kind invitation to take my meals with your family tomorrow?

ROBERT. You have been invited, so you must comply. My father would be upset otherwise.

BOTTWINK. If you insist.

ROBERT. If I am going to preside over the festivities, I'd better have a word with Briggs about what we are going to drink. We are to toast in Christmas on the strike of midnight.

BOTTWINK. And I would like to meet Lady Camilla.

ROBERT. Oh? Why, may I ask?

BOTTWINK. I am fascinated by the landed gentry in this country.

ROBERT. Really? You must excuse me.

ROBERT EXITS. ENTER LADY CAMILLA

CAMILLA. You must be Dr Bottwink. I am Lady Camilla. I am so glad you are to be with us over Christmas. It's going to be pretty bloody, but without you it will only be worse, with Robert in his present mood.

BOTTWINK. Worse, Lady Camilla? I do not understand. How could it be worse, seeing that it is I who will most likely be the offender in his eyes?

CAMILLA. Oh, don't imagine that you are the only one! He hates Sir Julius every bit as much because he thinks he is one of his own clan who has gone over to the other side. And he can't stand Mrs Carstairs either, for the same reason.

BOTTWINK. And you, my lady? Does he hate you also? And for what reason, if so?

CAMILLA. That is what I came down here to find out. We have, an understanding – I think.

BOTTWINK. I see. It would distress Lord Warbeck, would it not, if I were to refuse his hospitality?

CAMILLA. It would upset him very much. This Christmas gathering was entirely his idea, and he's not likely to have another. He is a very ill man, you understand. His doctors told him he would not see Christmas. An opinion he is determined to prove wrong.

BOTTWINK. What ails Lord Warbeck exactly?

CAMILLA. He's waiting for an aneurysm to blow up, or whatever aneurysms do.

BOTTWINK. I owe a great deal to his lordship. I will join your party over Christmas, Lady Camilla.

CAMILLA. Thank you. I am really grateful for that.

BOTTWINK. All the same, I fear that at the best I shall be somewhat of a fish out of water. Apart from being the object of Mr Robert's displeasure, there is so little in common between me and my fellow guests.

CAMILLA. I'm sure you could get on with anyone.

BOTTWINK. It is not so. I have rather specialised attainments. I had looked forward to meeting your Chancellor of the Exchequer – because there are certain points of constitutional theory and history affecting his office on which I fancied he could enlighten me. Did you know, for example, that a Chancellor of the Exchequer cannot sit in the House of Lords -

CAMILLA. Do you really expect a Cabinet Minister to know the first thing about constitutional history? He's much too busy running his department to bother about things like that. And besides, he hates talking shop.

BOTTWINK. I see.

CAMILLA. No, if you want to draw him out, try golf or fishing. Those are the only subjects he's really keen about.

BOTTWINK. Golf and fishing. Thank you, Lady Camilla. I shall remember. Perhaps with your assistance I shall even understand English public life at last!

CAMILLA. I can't guarantee that.

BOTTWINK. Tell me about Mrs Carstairs.

CAMILLA. What is there to say? She is the sort of woman one needn't listen to. So long as one looks intelligent, she'll go on all day talking about her marvellous husband without expecting one to answer. She is a bore. At the same time, there is something admirable in a woman's devotion to her husband – such a woman is lucky to have found a purpose in life. Her husband is tipped to be the next Chancellor, you know.

BOTTWINK. Really?

CAMILLA. When the present one decides to move over.

BOTTWINK. And what of Mr Robert? Does he deserve a woman's devotion?

CAMILLA. One may not agree with Robert's politics, but that's no reason for abusing him.

BOTTWINK. So you hope to capture his heart?

CAMILLA. I mean to have it out with him one way or the other. I can't go on like this – I simply can't. If he doesn't want me, let him just say so to my face.

BOTTWINK. Proud words from a proud woman.

CAMILLA. I'm sorry. I had no right to burden you like this. (*She looks out the window*) And just look at that snow! It's coming down as if it would never stop. It would be pretty bloody if we were all cooped for days and days. All we need then is a murder to keep us all occupied.

BOTTWINK. If you will excuse me, Lady Camilla. I must try and seek out Sir Julius.

CAMILLA. Certainly.

CAMILLA EXITS. ENTER SIR JULIUS

BOTTWINK. Ah, Sir Julius, we meet at last. I recognise you from the papers -

JULIUS. *(Ignoring him)* Tea! It's what one needs on a cold day like this! If I had my Sergeant Rogers here, he would organise tea immediately.

BOTTWINK. Indeed!

JULIUS. And you must be Dr Bottwink. My cousin told me you were here, rummaging among the papers. I hope you find something of interest.

BOTTWINK. Constitutional history is my speciality Sir Julius. Britain may not have a written constitution, but its history is steeped in the unwritten sort.

JULIUS. Quite! Quite! Now, where is my Sergeant? I expect he's checking out the kitchen staff.

BOTTWINK. You mention Lord Warbeck. Will he be dining with us tomorrow?

JULIUS. I doubt it. I understand Robert is to be our host for the festivities. I just hope the wine cellar is up to it.

BOTTWINK. I must admit, having Mr Robert here is somewhat disheartening.

JULIUS. I couldn't agree more. This League of Liberty of his is an affront to every thinking man and woman in this country who cares for democracy. Fortunately, we have the ladies to keep us off the subject of politics. At least we have Mrs Carstairs, which is indeed a pleasure. I have just been reading a masterly paper from her husband who is doing sterling work for us in Washington – most masterly.

BOTTWINK. Would that be Alan Carstairs?

JULIUS. It would indeed. Carstairs has the finest financial brain in Parliament – in the country even – even greater than my own - but never mind, his time will come. Every dog has his day, and we are all mortal.

BOTTWINK. Indeed we are, Sir Julius.

JULIUS. I know he lusts after my job in the Government, but he must be patient. That's the golden rule in politics. Now please, excuse me. I must organise some tea!

BOTTWINK. And I shall seek out Mrs Carstairs.

JULIUS EXITS. ENTER MRS CARSTAIRS

BOTTWINK. Ah, Mrs Carstairs, I presume. We have not had chance to speak.

CARSTAIRS. *(Looking out of the window)* Just look at that snow! I have to get up early tomorrow to go to church -

BOTTWINK. I fear that may prove to be impossible. From my observation, I should say that the snow will prevent anybody from going to church or anywhere else tomorrow morning.

CARSTAIRS. It's no distance to church. Surely we can have the path cleared as far as that?

BOTTWINK. I fear not.

CARSTAIRS. I just hope we don't have to suffer the prospect of playing bridge with Sir Julius. He always has difficulty with the scores. Really, for a Chancellor of the Exchequer –

BOTTWINK. One doesn't have to be a genius at arithmetic to handle the finances of the State, thank heaven! Why, there was one of Sir Julius' predecessors who didn't even know what a decimal point was, and when he saw one for the first time –

CARSTAIRS. Yes, yes, I am sure everyone has heard that story. And I may say it has been the stock excuse of inefficient Chancellors ever since.

BOTTWINK. Inefficient! Upon my soul, that is about the last thing I should have ever expected to hear applied to Sir Julius, especially from such a source as you, Mrs Carstairs! I understood your husband to be a loyal friend and colleague of Sir Julius.

CARSTAIRS. Yes, my husband *is* loyal! Too loyal to consider his own interests! I only hope the interests of the country do not suffer on account of my husband's sense of loyalty. In my position, my lips are sealed.

BOTTWINK. *(Checking his watch)* Are we not to gather soon for a Christmas toast? I do believe it is nearly midnight.

THEY ALL GATHER

ROBERT. *(Is drunk)* Thank you all for being here! *(He turns to Camilla)* Ah, Camilla, my dear. Tell me how much you care for me. What a beautiful nature you must have! A pity it should all be wasted, isn't it? But please don't stand on ceremony –

BOTTWINK. Mr Robert, I fear you are drunk. Perhaps –

ROBERT. Perhaps nothing! It only wants a few minutes to midnight. We already have the champagne to drink in the festive season, according to custom. According to custom! That's rich! But never mind! Let's keep up tradition while we may! The last Christmas in the old home – thanks to Cousin Julius and his band of socialist robbers!

BOTTWINK. I beg your pardon?

ROBERT. Don't you understand, when the old man dies, everything will go on death duties? Being lord of this particular pile of bricks will be a burden and no mistake. So, pick up your glasses and drink. *(He turns around)* glasses, Briggs, and give yourself one too. It is almost time. There's a tradition at stake! *(Robert listens)* Listen! Can't you hear them? Come close to the window, everybody! Closer! Camilla! Briggs! Come on, Julius! Can you hear them now?

THEY ALL MOVE TOWARDS THE WINDOW. CHURCH BELLS CAN BE HEARD

ROBERT. Warbeck chimes! Ringing in Christmas, ringing out the Warbecks! Except for fat old Julius, who'll always come out on top whatever happens! Now, listen, everybody! I've got an announcement to make – an important announcement! You mustn't miss it! (*He turns to Camilla*) Camilla! It's – it's – but it's Christmas! We must have our toast first! Where's my glass? Briggs, you fool, where the hell have you put my glass? (*He takes his glass*) Ah, here it is! Are you all ready? Here's to Warbeck Hall, God help the old place!

THE CHURCH BELLS STRIKE TWELVE AS ROBERT DRINKS. HE THEN CHOKES AND STAGGERS OFF STAGE, FOLLOWED BY BOTTWINK. AFTER A PAUSE, BOTTWINK ENTERS AND ADDRESSES THE AUDIENCE

BOTTWINK. Mr Robert - I am afraid he is quite dead. This is indeed shocking business for us all. But a moment! A sudden death has occurred here. A violent death. It is inevitable – is it not – that it must be followed by police enquiries. I understand we have the good fortune to have a police officer close to hand. (*He turns to Julius*) Sir Julius, I suggest you summon your Sergeant Rogers.

FADE

TWO

ENTER SERGEANT ROGERS AND SIR JULIUS

JULIUS. Ah, Sergeant Rogers.

ROGERS. Are you all right, sir? I was told I was wanted at once, and I thought -

JULIUS. Robert Warbeck has died, after drinking a glass of champagne.

ROGERS. This is a very unfortunate situation, sir. I am in some difficulty as to the proper procedure. This is a matter, which should be reported at once to the local police.

JULIUS. I quite agree.

ROGERS. As you know, sir, I am here simply on protection duty. So long as nothing happens to you, I am not concerned, strictly speaking. The investigation of an affair of this nature is entirely outside my sphere.

JULIUS. Very well, then, if that is the position, get in touch with the local police at once.

ROGERS. I beg your pardon, sir, but that is exactly the trouble. I thought you knew. It is impossible to communicate with the police station or with anybody outside the house. I tried to put through my routine report this evening, and the telephone was dead. The wireless reported that lines were down all over the country. We are completely cut off.

JULIUS. Cut off? But this is absurd! You know as well as I do that I must keep in touch with the Treasury at a time like this, Christmas or no Christmas. How is the country's business to be carried on – I'd like to know – if I am to be cut off, as you call it?

ROGERS. I could not say, sir. But the facts are as I have stated.

JULIUS. If that is really the case, you must do the best you can. You are a police officer, after all.

ROGERS. You wish me to undertake this enquiry, sir?

JULIUS. Until you can hand it over to the proper authorities – yes.

ROGERS. Very good, sir. When did death occur?

JULIUS. At twelve o'clock exactly. The clock was striking the precise moment.

ROGERS. Was everyone here present when the deceased died?

JULIUS. Oh, yes, certainly, everybody.

ROGERS. Very good. Now has anything in the room been touched since the death?

JULIUS. No, I think not.

ROGERS. Then I shall require a statement from everyone present.

JULIUS. But you're not proposing to take statements from us at this hour of the night, surely? I am not asking for any consideration for myself, but I should have thought it obvious that there were ladies here who should be spared such an ordeal.

ROGERS. You said just now that Mr Warlock died after drinking a glass of champagne. How long after?

JULIUS. Immediately! One might say that death came to him in the act of drinking.

ROGERS. Apparently as the result of what he drank?

JULIUS. Unquestionably. The champagne was poisoned.

ROGERS. Did anyone else drink from the same bottle?

JULIUS. All of us, I believe. I certainly did myself.

ROGERS. Thank you. I am now going to ask each of you to submit to a search.

JULIUS. Really, Sergeant! Why should this be necessary?

ROGERS. For a very plain reason, sir. If the deceased was poisoned, and the poison was not in the bottle from which he drank, it follows that somebody must have brought it into this room.

JULIUS. Good God! Do you imagine that I, for example –

ROGERS. It is not my business to imagine things, Sir Julius, but you desired me to undertake this enquiry and I must carry it out in the proper way. Do you mind turning out your pockets, sir?

JULIUS. Very well, if you insist. Though it seems to me ridiculous to suppose – how do you know that this wretched young man didn't poison himself?

JULIUS TURNS OUT HIS POCKETS

ROGERS. Thank you, Sir Julius.

JULIUS. I will be in my room if you need me.

JULIUS EXITS. ENTER DR BOTTWINK

ROGERS. You must be Dr Bottwink. I understand you are conducting historical research her at Warbeck Hall?

BOTTWINK. Indeed, I appear to have been caught up in an unfortunate situation. Have you any news to report, Sergeant.

ROGERS. I have examined the clothing of the deceased. So far as I am able to tell at present, there are no traces of poison on his person.

BOTTWINK. That is to be expected, is it not? A lethal dose of this poison is, after all, a very small amount.

ROGERS. What I am looking for is anything that could have served as a container. So far, I have failed to find it. Barring accident, which seems most improbable, this is a case either of suicide or murder. And for the time being, I am compelled to act upon the assumption that it is a case of murder. If it is, it was obviously committed by one of the people here present. And, in the circumstances, there is one obvious inquiry, which I must make.

BOTTWINK. I follow. Before we retire to rest, you wish to search our bedrooms to see if any of us has a supply of cyanide concealed in the wardrobe.

ROGERS. Why do you say cyanide?

BOTTWINK. I am not a medical doctor, but I have seen its use in the past.

ROGERS. Tell me, would there be a supply of cyanide in the house?

BOTTWINK. You must ask Briggs, the butler.

ROGERS. Ah, Briggs the butler. There is something else I must ask him.

ENTER BRIGGS

ROGERS. Ah, Briggs. I understand from the kitchen staff that you and Mr Robert were having words earlier this evening.

BRIGGS. About the wine for this evening.

ROGERS. It seemed more heated than that.

BRIGGS. I really don't see –

ROGERS. You were both talking about someone called Susan.

BRIGGS. Susan is my daughter.

ROGERS. And what of this promise Mr Robert was supposed to have made?

BRIGGS. Mr Robert was to have spoken to His Lordship on a personal matter.

ROGERS. It would appear the word 'threaten' was used. The word 'blackmail' was also used.

BRIGGS. Blackmail is not a term I would use.

ROGERS. Is there something between Mr Robert and your daughter, Briggs?

BRIGGS. I couldn't say.

ROGERS. Your daughter, is she here in the house?

BRIGGS. She is.

ROGERS. I shall have to speak to her, in due course.

BRIGGS. Is it cyanide of potassium you're looking for, Sergeant Rogers?

ROGERS. Yes.

BRIGGS. I've only just remembered. I have some in my pantry. It's in a little cupboard next to the sink. It's not locked. I got it for the wasps' nest last summer, and it's been there ever since. Would you like to see it?

ROGERS. You had better show it to me right away.

BRIGGS. Very good, Sergeant. I will go and fetch the cyanide immediately.

ROGERS. Tell me, when would you have gone to the cupboard last?

BRIGGS. I really couldn't say for sure. It isn't often I go there – it's just got a few odds and ends one doesn't often want. (*He pauses*) Wait a minute, though – I remember now, earlier today Dr Bottwink was showing me a bit of old panelling he'd found at the back of it. He was very interested in it, though it's nothing to look at.

ROGERS. I suppose the bottle was marked "poison"?

BRIGGS. That's right. A little blue bottle with "Poison" on the label in big letters

ROGERS. At least we know what to look for. Oh, by the way, how many rooms are there in this house?

BRIGGS. I've never counted them, but the guidebook says fifty-three.

ROGERS. Fifty-three. And if the poison bottle is not in the cupboard, it could be in any one of fifty-three rooms. If it's in the house at all, that is.

BRIGGS. I will go and check the cupboard. (*He stops*) His lordship! Who's going to break this to his lordship?

ROGERS. I suggest you break the news to him immediately. I shall meet you in the kitchen.

Murder Mysteries Vol 2

ROGERS EXITS. BOTTWINK TURNS TO BRIGGS

BOTTWINK. I have spent Christmas in many countries but this is the first time that I have actually been snowed up. And now there's thick fog, I understand. I take it that we are still cut off from the outside world?

BRIGGS. Yes. We are in a hollow here and the snow has drifted many feet deep.

BOTTWINK. How long will this go on, I wonder?

BRIGGS. Not very long, I hope. There is some prospect of a thaw setting in. A day or two should see the end of it.

BOTTWINK. A day or two! That can be a very long time in certain situations.

BRIGGS. Quite so.

BOTTWINK. Perhaps you are asking the same question as I am?

BRIGGS. Pardon?

BOTTWINK. The question that is exercising my mind is whether we shall all of us live to see the end of it. And you needn't look so shocked, Briggs. One must be realistic in matters of this sort. The cupboard containing the cyanide was empty, was it not? That means somebody is at large in this house with a supply of poison – an individual who may well choose to employ it again.

BRIGGS. Will you be needing me further?

BOTTWINK. No, you had better go and speak to your master. I hope he is not completely prostrated by the news.

BRIGGS. I don't know if I should tell him.

BOTTWINK. Really, Briggs! Now is not the time to stand of formality.

BRIGGS. It's not like that at all. If there's anyone in the world who's got the right to speak to his lordship about such a thing, I reckon that I have. It was just that when it comes to the point – when I see his lordship lying there, tired and weak -

BOTTWINK. It must be a very difficult moment for you. But all the same, we must face the fact that he has to be told some time. He will no doubt be expecting his son to come and see him soon.

BRIGGS EXITS. ENTER SIR JULIUS

JULIUS. Dr Bottwink, you are a foreigner.

BOTTWINK. I am bound to admit that that is so, Sir Julius.

JULIUS. I want to make clear that this unfortunate occurrence we witnessed was not in any way typical of our English way of life. In fact, I think it would be fairly described as entirely un-English. It is particularly painful to me to think that any foreigner should have been present at such a moment. The last thing in the world that I should desire would be for you to imagine that this shocking business was anything but quite exceptional.

BOTTWINK. It is well we are in England. In less favoured countries anything of this nature might be expected to have a political flavour – repercussions, even. But perhaps I should not have said that. Your own position, Sir Julius, must, of course, be, to some extent affected by the death of the heir to your cousin.

JULIUS. I beg your pardon!

BOTTWINK. You must forgive me if I fail to make myself clear. You see, as the good Sergeant Rogers put it, Mr Robert appears to have been murdered. That being so, the suspects are, conveniently, from a police point of view, extremely few. We have to choose between a Cabinet Minister, a young lady of the aristocracy, the wife of a rising politician, a trusted family servant and a foreigner of mixed parentage and doubtful nationality. To affect the arrest of any of the first three would clearly provoke a scandal of the first magnitude. To nab – I believe that is the word – to nab a family butler would shake the faith of the British public in one of their most cherished institutions. How fortunate, then, that there should be ready to hand a scapegoat for whom nobody in England would possibly care a brass farthing!

JULIUS. You are talking nonsense! And pernicious nonsense at that! I resent very deeply the suggestion that the police in this country would allow themselves to be influenced in any way –

BOTTWINK. Of course, it may not come to an arrest. Perhaps the good Sergeant will be unable to fix the blame upon any one individual among us five. We shall all of us then remain to some extent under a cloud for the rest of our lives. In which case, you will admit, that in your peculiarly vulnerable position, particularly when in due course you will succeed to the title of Lord Warbeck, it will be an advantage to you to be able to silence whispers by pointing to such an obviously disreputable and suspicious character as myself.

JULIUS. I refuse to listen to any more of this rubbish!

JULIUS EXITS. ENTER MRS CARSTAIRS

CARSTAIRS. Dr Bottwink. I am *so* glad to see you. I have been racking my brains to think of what could have possessed that poor young man to kill himself. Can it have been on account of some young woman, do you suppose? And yet when one thinks of Camilla, obviously head over heels in love with him –

BOTTWINK. You think Mr Robert committed suicide?

CARSTAIRS. But he must have, must he not? After all, we were all there. We saw him.

BOTTWINK. We saw him die.

CARSTAIRS. That is the same thing. I mean, any other suggestion would be too shocking!

BOTTWINK. Because a suggestion is shocking, it is not necessarily untrue.

CARSTAIRS. Do you believe that Robert was the victim of a hideous crime?

BOTTWINK. That is for Sergeant Rogers to judge.

CARSTAIRS. But seriously, Dr Bottwink, you can't possibly think that one of us could have
—

BOTTWINK. When I am told I cannot possibly think anything, my nature is so contradictory that I immediately begin to think about it. Have you not found that in your own experience?

CARSTAIRS. Certainly not! Quite clearly this was a case of suicide. Any other suggestion is simply not to be entertained. After all, as I have already pointed out, we were there. We saw what happened. We are the sole witnesses. Nobody else will be in a position to contradict what we say.

BOTTWINK. You obviously wish to hush this thing up. Well, I shall not stand in your way, though I cannot promise to assist. After all, this is no affair of mine. I have not been taught the English way of life. You may put wool on the eyes of Sergeant Rogers, if you can. Only I should warn you that you will not find the Sergeant as stupid as you think.

CARSTAIRS EXITS. ENTER SGT ROGERS

ROGERS. Dr Bottwink, may I ask you a personal question?

BOTTWINK. Of course, I am entirely at your service.

ROGERS. Tell me, what exactly are your political affiliations?

BOTTWINK. I am, of course, on the left. My leftism is a natural consequence of being pushed around from one country to another. We live in turbulent times.

ROGERS. Would it be fair to say you are a communist, Dr Bottwink?

BOTTWINK. I will not waste your time, Sergeant. There are two things you ought to know about me. One: I am opposed to the League of Liberty, Two: I did not, for that or any other reason, kill Mr Robert Warbeck.

ROGERS. This bottle of poison in the pantry cupboard, describe it to me. What did it look like?

BOTTWINK. I have not the least idea.

ROGERS. Are you telling me that it wasn't there?

BOTTWINK. I have no reason to doubt it that it was there. Merely I did not observe it.

ROGERS. You went twice to this cupboard, I understand. Once when you examined an old bit of woodwork – and again when you showed it to Briggs. Do you mean to say that on neither occasion you noticed what must have been right under your nose?

BOTTWINK. I was interested in the cupboard – or, to be more accurate, the old panelling in the back of the cupboard – and not in its contents. I am a historian, Sergeant, not a poisoner.

ROGERS. And you did not go back to the cupboard a third time?

BOTTWINK. Certainly not! I had no occasion to do so.

ROGERS. *(Takes out a twist of paper from his pocket)* Tell me, Doctor, have you seen this before?

BOTTWINK. *(Examines the twist)* No, I have not. What is it?

ROGERS. That will be for the analyst to say – when I can get hold of an analyst.

BOTTWINK. Quite so! May I ask where it was found?

ROGERS. Under the card table.

BOTTWINK. I see. That would, of course, be consistent with somebody having emptied the contents of this paper into Mr Robert's glass while it stood on the table, whether that somebody was himself or another. If it was another, we were all so occupied that it might have been done without it being noticed. On the other hand, if he did it himself – but, Sergeant, need we keep up this farce any longer?

ROGERS. What do you mean?

BOTTWINK. I mean that you do not believe, any more than I believe, that this unfortunate individual destroyed himself.

ROGERS. I –

BOTTWINK. Does a man, however drunken, declare in public that he is about to make an important announcement and then take poison before he can deliver it? It is absurd. You have already reached the conclusion that Robert Warbeck was murdered. Is that not so, Sergeant?

ROGERS. I am not here to answer your questions, Dr Bottwink.

BOTTWINK. As you please. But one question I should like answered very much, because it puzzles me. Have you found out what was the announcement Mr Robert was about to make?

ROGERS. I am not going to tell you that either.

BOTTWINK. A pity. If I knew that, it would perhaps help me to help you, and, believe me, I should like to help you if I could.

ROGERS. You can help me by answering one more question. Have you seen Lord Warbeck since the death of his son?

BOTTWINK. No, of course not. Why do you ask, Sergeant?

ROGERS. Somebody visited his lordship in his room between the time of his sons' death and now and that somebody had broken to him the news of his son's demise. When Briggs went into him just now, he found Lord Warbeck in a state of complete collapse.

BOTTWINK. And so is he dead, the poor fellow?

ROGERS. No. He is still alive, but no more than just alive. If you excuse me, I must speak to Sir Julius immediately.

BOTTWINK. Of course.

BOTTWINK EXITS AS SIR JULIUS ENTERS

JULIUS. Sergeant. Have you any news for me?

ROGERS. No, Sir Julius. I have tried the telephone again, but it is still dead. We shall soon hear the weather report on the wireless and then we shall perhaps know how long these conditions are to last. They can't go on much longer.

JULIUS. I must get in touch with the Prime Minister at Chequers at the earliest possible moment. That is essential. I'm in a most difficult predicament, Sergeant – most difficult.

ROGERS. Quite, sir.

JULIUS. Lady Camilla tells me that my cousin is in a very bad way.

ROGERS. Yes, sir. It would be interesting to know who it was who gave him the news that caused his collapse.

JULIUS. One of those damn fool servants, I suppose. They have no tact. If I had been left to break it to him, it might have been different. It is a terrible affair – terrible.

ROGERS. Quite, sir.

JULIUS. You wouldn't understand, but I am very deeply concerned about Lord Warbeck's condition.

ROGERS. It is only natural that you should be, sir. But you must remember that my concern at the moment is with Mr Robert Warbeck's death.

JULIUS. But I thought that was settled. He killed himself.

ROGERS. Unfortunately, Sir Julius, I have reason not to be satisfied with that explanation.

JULIUS. I know what it is. You've been listening to that damned Bottwink fellow.

ROGERS. Now, sir, suppose we start from the beginning and see if we can't get at the truth?

JULIUS. Very well, then. But I have given you a full and accurate account of everything that occurred, as far as my observation went. I have nothing else to tell you.

ROGERS. Nothing, Sir Julius?

JULIUS. Absolutely nothing.

ROGERS. Tell me, Sir Julius, on Mr Robert Warbeck's death you stand next in succession to the peerage. Is that correct?

JULIUS. Of course it's correct. But who do you suppose wants to be a peer nowadays? Especially in my position.

ROGERS. Did you know Briggs kept cyanide of potassium in the pantry?

JULIUS. Certainly not! I shouldn't know the stuff if I saw it.

ROGERS. I see. Thank you, Sir Julius.

JULIUS. This Bottwink chap, isn't he a communist?

ROGERS. He does not admit to being one, Sir Julius.

JULIUS. Of course he doesn't. Men of that sort never do. But given that he is, it could explain everything.

ROGERS. You mean that Mr Warbeck was killed because of his connection with the League of Liberty?

JULIUS. No! I was the person aimed at all the time! And the only thing that saved me was that in the confusion of the moment, the murderer put the poison in the wrong glass!

ROGERS. It is a theory, certainly, Sir Julius.

JULIUS. And now that his attempt has failed, Bottwink is trying to discredit me – and through me, the cause of freedom throughout the world! I ask you to imagine the effect on Western Democracy if I were to be suspected of murder!

ROGERS. I am bound to say, Sir Julius, that from what I have seen of Dr Bottwink, he seems to be more interested in eighteenth century politics than modern ones.

JULIUS. Eighteenth century fiddlesticks! I tell you, the man's a menace!

THEY BOTH EXIT. ENTER BOTTWINK AND LADY CAMILLA

BOTTWINK. Lady Camilla. Have you recovered from the shock?

CAMILLA. I know what people are thinking, Doctor.

BOTTWINK. And what is that?

CAMILLA. Robert treated me like a cad and that if anybody had a reason for killing him, I did. Robert used to be such a sweet person. How can such a man become so sour and bitter?

BOTTWINK. I cannot say. I daresay his involvement in the League of Liberty might have some bearing on his attitude.

CAMILLA. I wouldn't do anything to hurt him. I simply wanted him to understand.

BOTTWINK. Sometimes women want too much, especially from a man.

CAMILLA. Robert could be a hateful beast at times.

BOTTWINK. Love can turn to hate so quickly.

CAMILLA. Do you think he had another woman?

BOTTWINK. I really couldn't say.

CAMILLA. I'll tell you something else, up to two minutes to midnight I <u>was</u> wishing him dead. And now, I wish I was dead myself. Silly, isn't it?

BOTTWINK. You must not say things like that. Can't you see how dangerous that sort of talk can be?

CAMILLA. Dangerous?

BOTTWINK. If you were to say a thing like that to Sergeant Rogers -

CAMILLA. I almost admitted as much to the Sergeant earlier this evening.

BOTTWINK. *(Changing tack)* How is Lord Warbeck?

CAMILLA. There doesn't seem to be any change in him.

BOTTWINK. Who is staying with his lordship now?

CAMILLA. Briggs' daughter, Susan. I had quite forgotten that Briggs had any family.

BOTTWINK. I am sure she is quite capable of looking after his lordship.

CAMILLA. She would hardly be Briggs' daughter if she wasn't. But I have to tell you, she is also a dark horse. She looks so sweet as if butter wouldn't melt in her mouth. But she has some very dark ways, I can tell you.

BOTTWINK. I would very much like to speak to her.

CAMILLA EXITS. ENTER SUSAN BRIGGS

BOTTWINK. It's Susan, isn't it? We haven't met before, have we?

SUSAN. No, we haven't.

BOTTWINK. You don't live here then?

SUSAN. I only came down a day or two ago.

BOTTWINK. Briggs has kept you very quiet.

SUSAN. Dad didn't want anyone to know I was here. But I have a right to be here, which is more than some can say.

BOTTWINK. What is this right, you speak of?

SUSAN. Robert Warbeck and I were married. That's what I mean.

BOTTWINK. Thank you. It is a great pity nobody knew of this before. It might have made a difference to a good lot of people. You are quite right. You are entitled to be here.

SUSAN. Thank you.

BOTTWINK. Does Lady Camilla know of this marriage between yourself and Robert Warbeck?

SUSAN. She knows now. I told her earlier this evening. It's a funny thing, all this time I've been trying to get close enough to tell his lordship, and now I can, it's all over bar the shouting. Poor old man. He was nice. I expect he'd have been decent to me if Robert had done the proper thing. It seems a shame I can't tell him the one thing that might have cheered him up.

BOTTWINK. At least you have no more shocks in store for us.

SUSAN. What about my baby boy?

BOTTWINK. Baby boy?

SUSAN. Yes, Robert and I have a baby boy.

BOTTWINK. I think you have said enough for the time being.

FADE

THREE

ENTER BOTTWINK AND MRS CARSTAIRS

CARSTAIRS. How long will this go on for, do you suppose? One feels so utterly helpless, being isolated in this way.

BOTTWINK. I'm sure I couldn't say, Mrs Carstairs.

CARSTAIRS. But can't somebody do something about it? It seems so hopeless, just sitting here waiting for something to happen. Couldn't we organise – to *do* something?

BOTTWINK. Briggs tells me the farm workers are trying to get through to the village. They have made some progress down the lane but the snow is becoming soft and they are having great difficulty.

CARSTAIRS. Soft, did you say?

BOTTWINK. Yes. There is apparently some prospect of a thaw.

CARSTAIRS. Thank Heaven for that!

BOTTWINK. Widespread floods are now anticipated, according to the radio.

CARSTAIRS. How is Lord Warbeck?

BOTTWINK. Resting. There is someone looking after him. Briggs has been good enough to arrange that his daughter should sit with him.

CARSTAIRS. His daughter? I remember her. Why did nobody tell me she was here? As I recall, she went into service in London. Such a bright little thing, she was – but rather a handful! I wonder what became of her.

BOTTWINK. She married. Unfortunately she has recently been widowed.

CARSTAIRS. Dear me, how sad!

BOTTWINK. Indeed, I must speak to Miss Susan further.

CARSTAIRS. Then you must excuse me.

THEY EXIT. ENTER ROGERS AND SUSAN

ROGERS. (*To the audience*) I'm afraid I have some bad news. Lord Warbeck is dead. He went quite peacefully. (*he turns to Susan*) And this is Susan Briggs. She was with him when he died.

SUSAN. There was something else I have to tell you that's more important. You may be forgiven for thinking that now the old gentleman's dead Sir Julius will become the new Lord Warbeck. Well, he won't.

ROGERS. What do you mean?

SUSAN. Mr Robert was married to me, and my baby boy is therefore the rightful Lord Warbeck!

ROGERS. You have a son? Mr Robert's boy? Born in wedlock? Good Heavens! Did Lord Warbeck know about this?

SUSAN. No. It was scarcely a matter anyone could discuss with him. I was relying on Robert to put things right with his lordship. But it was a great mistake to rely on Robert for anything.

ROGERS. Do you have any more surprises for us?

SUSAN. You realise that now makes two of them. Robert locked away in the drawing room and his lordship in bed upstairs. There's now just us left - shut in by this fog and snow. Who'll be the next to go, do you suppose? I don't know about you, but I want to get away from here. I want to get away before it is too late. There is a curse on this house. It smells of death. We're not safe here – not one of us. Can't you feel that? Don't you understand that the longer we stay here –

ROGERS. As for staying here, it is unfortunately the case that we have no option in the matter until – the fog finally lifts and it starts to rain.

THEY EXIT. ENTER BOTTWINK AND LADY CAMILLA

BOTTWINK. I trust the library is watertight with the threat of flooding. It would be a major disaster to scholarship if anything were to happen to the manuscripts there.

CAMILLA. God, I'm tired. I'm going up to my room to lie down. I think I could sleep now.

BOTTWINK. I suppose we shall continue to call Sir Julius by his existing title and not Lord Warbeck. But no matter, you now live in an advanced democratic state and such things as titles and peerages are interesting relics of the past.

CAMILLA. I daresay as a democrat, Sir Julius might have found a peerage embarrassing.

BOTTWINK. I am, of course, aware that England has progressed in many ways. None the less, to an outsider like myself, it would appear that in some respects you are still gripped by the dead hand of the past. I encountered a most interesting example in my research, perhaps you would like to hear it? It appears that a Chancellor of the Exchequer cannot -

CAMILLA. You have already told me that, Doctor. You must excuse me.

THEY EXIT. ENTER ROGERS AND BRIGGS

ROGERS. You ought to have told me about this in the first place, Briggs.

BRIGGS. Yes, I quite see that now. But I'd got so in the habit of keeping quiet about it that it had almost become second nature with me, so to speak. You see, I looked on it as a matter between myself and Mr Robert.

ROGERS. Exactly. You thought that it was his duty to tell his father and to acknowledge your daughter as his wife?

BRIGGS. Just so.

ROGERS. And you had been threatening him with the consequences if he didn't do so?

BRIGGS. I don't like the use of the word threaten. There were some hard words between us, that I will admit. But if it comes to threats, what could I do? If the worst came to the worst, I could tell his lordship, but in his state of health I wasn't going to be the one to give him a shock that might have killed him.

ROGERS. You were very fond of Lord Warbeck, weren't you? And not particularly fond of his son?

BRIGGS. Robert did not act like a gentleman, and that's a fact.

ROGERS. May it be that you preferred killing the son rather than shocking your master?

BRIGGS. Just look what the shock of Mr Robert's death did to him, God rest him!

ROGERS. You will have an opportunity of making your explanation to the local police before very long. All right, Briggs, you can go for now. I suppose I had better talk to your daughter so as to have a complete picture.

BRIGGS. Very good. I will send her to you now.

ROGERS. Tell me something before you go. If this rain stops soon, how soon do you reckon anybody will be able to get through?

BRIGGS. It all depends on the stream you have to cross to get to the village. Last time we had snow like this we were cut off by floods for three days when the thaw came. I'm hopeful that we shall be in touch with the outside world by tomorrow.

THEY EXIT. ENTER BOTTWINK AND SIR JULIUS

JULIUS. I'm going out!

BOTTWINK. Out! But Sir Julius, that's impossible!

JULIUS. Nonsense! One can't stay shut up in here forever. I want a breath of fresh air.

BOTTWINK. You will be up to your knees in water before you have gone a yard.

JULIUS. I shall borrow a pair of waders. Briggs will know where to find them. I shall stick to the drive. If I can, I shall make my way towards the village. I may even be able to get across the bridge and send for help. It's worth trying, anyway. At the worst, I shall have had some exercise.

BOTTWINK. You will be careful, won't you? After all that has happened, we can't face any more disasters. Not with a cabinet minister, anyway.

JULIUS. I can take care of myself.

BOTTWINK. And what of Sergeant Rogers?

JULIUS. I beg your pardon!

BOTTWINK. It's the Sergeants job to take care of you. Special Branch would not take it kindly if the Sergeant allowed you to go out on a day like this.

JULIUS. I'll do whatever I please. Dash it all, I'm not a babe in arms. I am entitled to go out for a walk by myself if I want to. If I had got drowned it would have been my own fault.

BOTTWINK. Your fault and the Sergeant's responsibility. You forget that. And suppose you had not been drowned? I'm not sure that wouldn't have been worse from the Sergeant's point of view. Suppose you had turned up in Downing Street tomorrow without your protector? There would have been a lot of awkward explaining to do.

JULIUS. *(Realising)* I suppose so.

BOTTWINK. Just as a matter of interest, Sir Julius. I suppose it was Downing Street you were making for?

JULIUS. Oh yes, it was Downing Street. I'm not a fugitive escaping from justice.

BOTTWINK. You must excuse me. I would like a word with Briggs.

JULIUS EXITS. ENTER BRIGGS

BOTTWINK. Mrs Carstairs has been gone a long time. Do you not find it strange?

BRIGGS. She took a tray of tea up to Lady Camilla's room. Has she not come down?

BOTTWINK. She has not come down.

BRIGGS. When she does come down, I will make a fresh pot of tea –

BOTTWINK. You consider that everything is to be made right by a pot of tea. Myself, I do not think so. Already some things have happened in this house that are not to be cured by pots of tea. Perhaps this is another. I do not know. I hope only that I may be wrong.

BRIGGS. What exactly are you getting at, Dr Bottwink?

BOTTWINK. I do not know what I am getting at, as you put it. Perhaps it is simply that my nerves are getting to me. Merely, I ask myself – where on earth can Mrs Carstairs be? Not to mention Lady Camilla herself? It seems strange to me, and in a household like this everything that is strange is alarming.

BRIGGS. You are very easily alarmed.

BOTTWINK. You are positive Mrs Carstairs took Lady Camilla her tea?

BRIGGS. Positive!

BOTTWINK. I have been told me more than once that I do not comprehend English ways and customs. It has also been pointed out to me that what has happened in this house has been quite un-English. However, the position, as I see it, is this: there is a killer abroad amongst us, who has already struck once – possibly twice. I have now determined in my own mind who that killer is, and if Sergeant Rogers had been content to follow my advice –

BRIGGS. If you will excuse me, I have work to attend to.

BRIGGS EXITS. ENTER SGT ROGERS

BOTTWINK. Sergeant Rogers, have you seen Mrs Carstairs and Lady Camilla?

ROGERS. There is no cause for alarm. Lady Camilla is asleep in her room and Mrs Carstairs is resting in hers.

BOTTWINK. Mrs Carstairs has told you this?

ROGERS. No, Briggs' daughter happened to be on the landing when Mrs Carstairs came out of her ladyship's room and that was the information she conveyed to her. She added that Lady Camilla was not to be disturbed.

BOTTWINK. I do not know what to say. I have been very foolish. I am ashamed. I shall go to the library now to continue my studies. I should never have left it. I am good for one thing only. It is a mistake to interfere in what is not one's business. This shall be a lesson to me.

ROGERS. Just a moment. I think you are forgetting that the matter that was worrying you in the first place has still to be cleared up.

BOTTWINK. I do not understand.

ROGERS. Briggs told me that you were concerned because Mrs Carstairs left our company and did not come back.

BOTTWINK. Ah, that! It was only because she had left with Lady Camilla that I was worried. I was not afraid for the safety of Lady Carstairs, no!

ROGERS. Well, I don't see why you should be concerned for the safety of one person more than another. My job is the safety of Sir Julius and I am not particularly interested in anybody else. But since we are here in this house, I think it would be as well to check on Mrs Carstair's room and make certain that she is all right too.

BOTTWINK. As you please, Sergeant. I repeat, it does not concern me.

ROGERS. Nevertheless, we will check on both ladies.

THEY BOTH EXIT

FADE

FOUR

ENTER BOTTWINK AND ROGERS

BOTTWINK. But no! It is impossible! By all the rules of logic and reason, it is impossible!

ROGERS. But it has happened. Mrs Carstairs is quite dead. Poisoned.

BOTTWINK. The thing is so absurd! Mrs Carstairs, of all people!

ROGERS. I don't understand you. If there is a maniac in this house going about murdering people, is there any reason why Mrs Carstairs should have been safer than anyone else?

BOTTWINK. If there is a maniac, then there is no reason for anything. That is logical. That I can comprehend. But I have seen no signs of mania here. On the contrary. I have assumed a murderer who is sane, and on that assumption there were just two people, two only, whose lives I was prepared to consider secure – Mrs Carstairs and Sir Julius. But now –

ROGERS. May I ask why you should choose to bring Sir Julius into the matter?

BOTTWINK. This is getting us nowhere. Let us stick to the facts. Mrs Carstairs has died, it would appear in exactly the same way Mr Robert Warbeck died – from cyanide poisoning.

ROGERS. An analysis will have to be made in due course, but all the evidence points to her having taken the poison in her tea. We know that there is a bottle of this poison somewhere in the house, but although I have searched her room thoroughly I have been unable to find it. In that case, the poison was in the tea before Mrs Carstairs brought it to Lady Camilla. Now, we know something of the history of that tea. It was made, not for Mrs Carstairs, but for Lady Camilla, and taken up to her room by the deceased. Apparently, it was only by chance that Lady Camilla was asleep and didn't want any tea which induced Mrs Carstairs to drink it herself.

BOTTWINK. But why would she have done that? Why didn't she return to us?

ROGERS. I am dealing simply with the facts. Thus it follows that if the tea was deliberately poisoned - it was intended to kill not Mrs Carstairs but Lady Camilla. Now the tea was freshly made in the kitchen – brought in by Briggs and handed to Mrs Carstairs. So far as we know, it never left her hands until she died.

BOTTWINK. Then you had better speak to Briggs.

BOTTWINK EXITS AS BRIGGS ENTERS

ROGERS. Briggs, you made the tea, did you not?

BRIGGS. Yes. I made it.

ROGERS. Was anybody else with you at the time?

BRIGGS. I was quite alone.

ROGERS. You had better tell the truth. Who was with you in the kitchen?

BRIGGS. My daughter was with me for part of the time.

ROGERS. What part did she take in the tea making?

BRIGGS. I was cutting the bread and butter at the kitchen table when my daughter came into the room. The kettle was on the range behind me and was just coming to the boil. She asked me who the tea was for and I told her. I'd warmed the pot and put the tea in it all ready. Then the kettle boiled and she asked me should she fill the pot. To save myself trouble, I told her, yes. I didn't so much as look around. She filled the pot and put it on the tray beside me and went out. That's all.

ROGERS. It was you who told us that Mrs Carstairs had taken the tea intended for Lady Camilla to her own room. You had that information from your daughter?

BRIGGS. Yes. I reported it to you just as she told me.

ROGERS. Your daughter seems to have been very much concerned in this affair.

BRIGGS. I can't believe that she had anything to do with it.

ROGERS. That is a matter she will have to explain to the proper authorities in due course. Where is she at the moment?

BRIGGS. Do you wish to see her?

ROGERS. Yes. Ask her to come here at once. And you are to tell her nothing of what has occurred, do you understand?

BRIGGS. Very good.

THEY EXIT. ENTER LADY CAMILLA AND BOTTWINK

BOTTWINK. Lady Camilla.

CAMILLA. Can I ask you a question?

BOTTWINK. Ask away.

CAMILLA. Why did you and Sergeant Rogers come into my room?

BOTTWINK. It was an unhappy misunderstanding on my part. And I am very happy that I was mistaken. Quite simply, when I came into your room, I thought you were dead.

CAMILLA. That's the oddest excuse I've ever heard for coming into a woman's room, and I've heard a good many.

BOTTWINK. It is true, none the less.

CAMILLA. And why should I have been dead in my room?

BOTTWINK. Mrs Carstairs is dead.

CAMILLA. Mrs Carstairs! Dead! How?

BOTTWINK. She has been poisoned, apparently from the tea which was prepared for you and which she drank herself because she found you asleep. I trust you were asleep when she came into your room?

CAMILLA. Did she come into my room? Certainly I was asleep if she did.

BOTTWINK. That is well. You will remember to tell the police that when they question you. But for now, I think Sergeant Rogers would like to speak to young Susan.

CAMILLA EXITS. ENTER SUSAN AND ROGERS

SUSAN. You wanted to see me, Sergeant.

ROGERS. I understand that you were in the kitchen just now when your father was making tea for Lady Camilla?

SUSAN. That's right.

ROGERS. He says that you helped him to make the tea. Is that so?

SUSAN. I filled the pot from the kettle, that's all. The kettle was boiling and Dad was cutting bread and butter and I offered to fill the pot. There was nothing wrong with the tea, was there?

ROGERS. There was poison in it.

SUSAN. Poison? In the tea that Dad made?

ROGERS. In the tea you made together.

SUSAN. But I never did anything, except put the boiling water in when Dad told me. What should I want to poison anyone for?

ROGERS. You knew that tea was for Lady Camilla, didn't you?

SUSAN. Has anything happened to her?

ROGERS. Nothing has happened to Lady Camilla. You know quite well that she did not drink the tea. Mrs Carstairs did.

SUSAN. Has anything happened to her, then?

ROGERS. Mrs Carstairs is dead.

SUSAN. Well, that's not my fault, is it?

ROGERS. What were you doing outside Lady Camilla's door?

SUSAN. I went up there because I wanted to talk to her.

ROGERS. What about?

SUSAN. We'd had words earlier when I went to sit in his lordship's room and I –

ROGERS. You wanted to have some more words with her, was that it?

SUSAN. It doesn't matter now. I didn't see her, anyway.

ROGERS. You went up there to see whether she had drunk the tea, didn't you?

SUSAN. I tell you, I didn't know anything about the tea. When I got there, Mrs Carstairs was just coming out of Lady Camilla's room. She said her ladyship was asleep and was not to be disturbed. We had some words and then she took the tea away to her room and I went off to mine. That's all!

ROGERS. You made no attempt to stop Mrs Carstairs taking the tea which you knew was intended for Lady Camilla?

SUSAN. Why should I? I tell you, I didn't know –

ROGERS. Very well, Mrs Warbeck. I don't think I need trouble you any further. You understand that other people may ask you questions about this later on?

SUSAN. They'll only get the same answers.

ROGERS. That should be all for now.

SUSAN EXITS. BOTTWINK AND ROGERS MOVE FORWARD

ROGERS. As I have said before, my business here is to protect Sir Julius. I do not regard myself as being in charge of this case. It cannot be long now before the local police arrive and it will be their business to carry out the investigations. But it puzzles me to think what motive the good Briggs' daughter should have to seek to poison Lady Camilla.

BOTTWINK. Motive enough - two women and one man.

ROGERS. That is motive enough, certainly. However, I am not concerned with theories. My function is simply to assemble all the facts that come under my notice and hand them over to the proper authorities. And yet there is one thing worthy of note. Mrs Carstairs shoes were wet. There were traces on the carpet which indicated that she had been to the French window in her room and had stepped out on to the balcony for a moment. There is a great deal of melting snow there still.

BOTTWINK. I am not a detective, but you seem to have established the fact that explains the condition, though not the reason that explains the fact.

ROGERS. True.

BOTTWINK. A question, Sergeant.

ROGERS. Go ahead.

BOTTWINK. That young woman, Susan, is the widow of the Honourable Mr Warbeck. How long have we known this?

ROGERS. Only since today.

BOTTWINK. And the others?

ROGERS. Apart from Briggs, nobody knew of it until today. Sir Julius learned of it only after Lord Warbeck's death.

BOTTWINK. And the ladies?

ROGERS. Only Lady Camilla was told.

BOTTWINK. I see.

ROGERS. Excuse me, I must speak with Sir Julius.

BOTTWINK EXITS. ENTER SIR JULIUS

JULIUS. *(Carrying a bottle of poison)* Sergeant! Look at this! I found it in my wardrobe. In the drawer where I keep my handkerchiefs! I went to get myself a clean one just now, and when I picked it up, there this was, lying just underneath! It's the poison! What do you think of that?

ROGERS. *(Examines the bottle)* Empty, I see.

JULIUS. Well? Isn't that the thing you're looking for?

ROGERS. It seems so, Sir Julius. Briggs will be able to identify it, no doubt.

JULIUS. And it was in my wardrobe, of all places. How the devil did it get there, do you suppose?

ROGERS. Well, sir, your room is readily accessible from the stairs. Once on the landing, it is the first door one comes to.

JULIUS. Quite. Next door to Lady Camilla's, in fact. Mrs Carstairs' room is just beyond.

ROGERS. I have that in mind, sir.

JULIUS. You searched their rooms, I suppose?

ROGERS. Yes, sir.

JULIUS. Then, how –

ROGERS. I have no suggestion to offer, sir. And unless the person who put this bottle in your wardrobe chooses to tell us, I see no means of finding out.

JULIUS. I suppose I should have left it where it was until you could see it.

ROGERS. You should, sir.

JULIUS. There might have been fingerprints on it, and so on.

ROGERS. There *was* the possibility of fingerprints, certainly.

JULIUS. I am sorry. It was stupid of me. I'm afraid I rather lost my head when I saw it there.

ROGERS. I quite understand, sir. No doubt the officer who takes charge of this case in due course will accept your explanation, in view of your position.

JULIUS. Good God, Sergeant, I should hope so!

ROGERS. He will, of course, have to take account of the fact that there is no corroboration of your statement of how this was found.

JULIUS. What!

ROGERS. However, there is one point as to which I shall be able to satisfy him. It was not in your wardrobe when I searched it earlier.

JULIUS. At least there is one point in which we can take comfort.

ROGERS. Oh!

JULIUS. The bottle is now empty. It means that we can drink our coffee here with some degree of confidence.

THEY EXIT. ENTER BOTTWINK AND SUSAN

BOTTWINK. Ah, Mrs Warbeck. I wonder if I could ask you a question?

SUSAN. *(Upset)* I'm not saying anything. I've told the Sergeant everything that happened.

BOTTWINK. May I assure you that the question is not one put to you already by the Sergeant.

SUSAN. I'm still not saying anything.

BOTTWINK. I implore you to assist. We are all of us under a shadow here. It rests with you to deliver us. A simple statement that can in no way incriminate you –

SUSAN. What's with all this badgering and bothering? There's not a person in this house that hasn't been at me sooner or later, and now you have to start! Why can't you all leave me alone?

BOTTWINK. Did Mrs Carstairs badger and bother you?

SUSAN. She was the worst of the lot!

BOTTWINK. That was when you met her outside Lady Camilla's door, no doubt?

SUSAN. What do you know about that?

BOTTWINK. Nothing. Tell me about Mrs Carstairs' badgering and bothering, and I think I can promise you that you will neither be badgered or bothered again.

SUSAN. What's it got to do with you?

BOTTWINK. You and she had words, did you not?

SUSAN. It was all her fault if we did.

BOTTWINK. Naturally. I am not suggesting otherwise.

SUSAN. It was she who began it.

BOTTWINK. Of course.

SUSAN. I shouldn't have said a word if she hadn't tried to come the high and mighty over me.

BOTTWINK. No doubt you were greatly provoked.

SUSAN. Well, you could hardly blame me for speaking my mind, could you?

BOTTWINK. Certainly not!

SUSAN. I told her straight. "I'm not to be treated as a nobody. I expect to be spoken to respectful." The impertinence of it! Her asking me what I was doing outside her ladyship's door! I've a right to go where I like in this house, haven't I?

BOTTWINK. I should be the last to deny it of you.

SUSAN. She said she wondered what the girls of today were coming to, and did I remember who I was speaking to. "I am the Honourable Mrs Warbeck," I said, "and what's more, my little boy is the rightful Lord Warbeck now his grandfather's dead."

BOTTWINK. And the boy, is he with you now?

SUSAN. That's what she wanted to know, only she didn't put it like that. "Where is this brat?" She said. That's what she called my son, a brat. "Safe at home with his auntie," I said, "where nobody can get at him." And then she looked at me so fierce, if she hadn't had the tea tray in her hands I believe she'd have gone for me.

BOTTWINK. Yes, yes, quite so. Pray continue.

SUSAN. Well, that's all that happened, really. She hadn't a word to say after that. I mean, how could she? She just turned away, leaving me standing where I was, and went down the passage to her own room. When she gets to her own door she turns round and says, "I shall have my tea in my own room," she says, "and please understand that Lady Camilla is asleep and is not to be disturbed." Then she goes into her room and shuts the door and that's the last I see of her.

BOTTWINK. Thank you, Mrs Warbeck. I should explain to you – *(a phone bell rings)* God bless my soul! If it's not the telephone! We finally have communication with the outside world.

SUSAN. Thank heaven this nightmare is over. Can I go now?

BOTTWINK. Certainly.

SUSAN EXITS. ENTER SGT ROGERS

ROGERS. The police will be here in a few hours, if all goes well. The road is clear as far as Warbeck village.

BOTTWINK. And when they come, what do you propose to tell them, may I ask?

ROGERS. I have already told you. I do not consider myself as being in charge of this case any longer. I shall simply place my report in their hands and leave the matter to them.

BOTTWINK. Your report – just so. Is it in a state of completion?

ROGERS. It is not altogether complete. But it will be very shortly. I have only a few additional facts to add so as to bring it up to date. Unless, of course, you can tell us who killed Mr Robert.

BOTTWINK. Of course I know who killed Mr Robert. And Lord Warbeck. And Mrs Carstairs. It was all one and the same person.

ROGERS. I think you had better explain.

BOTTWINK. Sir Julius has characterised the events we have witnessed as un-English. But I beg to differ. This crime could only have happened in England. It is, indeed, an essentially English Murder.

ROGERS. Why do you say this is an English Murder?

BOTTWINK. Because the motive was English. Because it was made possible by a political factor that is peculiar to England. This crime could not have occurred but for the fact that England retains in its constitution a hereditary legislative chamber – The House of Lords. And the murderer's motive was quite simply to procure a seat in that chamber for one person by removing the two individuals who stood between him and the right to occupy it.

ROGERS. I have never such nonsense in my life! Do you dare to suggest that Sir Julius –

BOTTWINK. The matter is a little more complicated than that. Constitutionally a Prime Minister may sit in the House of Lords, a Chancellor of the Exchequer, on the other hand, may not. Should Sir Julius succeed to the family peerage, he would have to vacate his present position. And in doing so, who would be the obvious successor to the position of Chancellor? I am no student of contemporary politics, but surely Mrs Carstairs' husband –

ROGERS. Alan Carstairs is the obvious man, certainly.

BOTTWINK. Precisely! There is the case in a nutshell. Need I insult your intelligence by saying any more? Your primary function, as you have more than once emphasised, was to protect Sir Julius. And you have performed it with efficiency. But there was one danger against which you were powerless to protect your charge – the danger of an unwelcome elevation to the House of Lords. Sir Julius owes his escape from that, not to Scotland Yard, but to the happy circumstances that there existed, unknown to us all, an infant Lord Warbeck.

ROGERS. Dr Bottwink, do I understand you to suggest that Mrs Carstairs murdered Mr Robert Warbeck?

BOTTWINK. She did.

ROGERS. And Lord Warbeck?

BOTTWINK. Certainly. That is to say, it was she who broke the news of his son's death with the intention of hastening his own. She was impatient.

ROGERS. Then will you tell me, who, in your view, killed Mrs Carstairs?

BOTTWINK. But I have answered that question already. Did I not say that one person was responsible for all three deaths? Mrs Carstairs, of course, killed herself.

ROGERS. Why on earth should she do that?

BOTTWINK. It is obvious, is it not? Once she discovered the infant heir to the Warbeck title, all her attempts to secure office for her husband were to fail. The mechanics of her suicide are for you to determine, but I would say that the state of her shoes and the marks upon her carpet would suggest that the poison was secreted in the snow, which until recently, was deep upon the balcony of her room. She recovered the bottle, emptied it into her tea and then, as a final gesture of contempt – or perhaps in the hope of casting suspicion upon Sir Julius that would blast his career as effectively as would a peerage – deposited it in his wardrobe. That done, she returned to her room, poured out the tea and so performed the last act of despair.

ROGERS. Sir Julius has had a close squeak, the next man may not be so lucky.

BOTTWINK. Let us go and have – what is it the English say? A nice cup of tea.

THEY EXIT

END OF PLAY

DEATH ON THE FRINGE

By John Dunne

Loosely adapted from the play by Sir Richard Parsons

Characters
Gill Partridge
Jane Shannon
Kate Portland-Brown
Tatiania Verona
Brian Russell
Andrew Fraser
Sir Emrys Merioneth
Inspector Stout

An interactive murder mystery ideal for dinner parties and social occasions. The script can be personalised for extra fun!

Welcome to *Death on the Fringe.* We are in the world of fringe theatre, dictatorial directors, precious playwrights and luvvie actors. We are also in the world of murder and deceit!

Gill Partridge and Jane Shannon are putting on a play. Entitled *Mounting Olympias,* the play features Alexander the Great, King Philip of Macedon, Queen Olympias and Eurydice, a docile local girl. The play also features Aristotle, a great sage played by the world famous Sir Emrys Merioneth – last seen playing God with Leonardo di Caprio in *Paradise Lost.*

This motley crew struggle to put on the play amidst bickering, jealousy, lust and envy. Something is bound to happen, and it does. Somebody gets murdered.

As guests for this evening, you are invited to participate in proceedings – both as possible suspects and sleuths. Be prepared to take part, be ready to stand in the breach – just don't tell Equity!

Murder Mysteries Vol 2

ONE

ENTER GILL PARTRIDGE AND JANE SHANNON

PARTRIDGE. I don't really care for authors. Don't usually let them into auditions. Or rehearsals. I only made an exception for you because you promised to keep quiet.

SHANNON. And I put up the money.

PARTRIDGE. A little money.

SHANNON. I'm not well paid at the museum, you know. But Aunt Marigold in Ilfracombe died just at the right moment. So like her to do the decent thing.

PARTRIDGE. You'll get it back. When this play of yours transfers to the West End.

SHANNON. *(Chuffed)* Do you think so?

PARTRIDGE. It'll be marvellous. By the time I've finished with the cutting.

SHANNON. *(Appalled)* Cutting!

PARTRIDGE. *(With relish)* Lots of cutting. In rehearsal.

SHANNON. Sounds more like an amputation. I do value every precious word, you know.

PARTRIDGE. Hard cheese. The punters won't sit through three hours.

SHANNON. They do for Ibsen.

PARTRIDGE. This isn't Ibsen. They won't want to be late away. Not in this neck of the woods. Fifteen minutes walk to the nearest train station. And don't forget, the music starts in the bar down below at nine-thirty. Horrible din.

SHANNON. *(Aghast)* But my play means so much to me. Like a fragile child one is letting loose on a hostile world.

PARTRIDGE. This is fringe theatre darling, be glad you're getting it on at all.

SHANNON. I offered my script to the National. RSC. The Royal Court. Everywhere.

PARTRIDGE. Never mind, you've got me. Artistic Director of the old Queen's Head.

SHANNON. *(Cheering up)* Off-Broadway, you might say.

PARTRIDGE. Sorry. This is the wrong end of town. Mind you, I do have a secret weapon that's going to put us both on the map. *(Checking her notes)* Now, where are these actors? Who's first on my list? Ah, Kate Portland-Brown.

Murder Mysteries Vol 2

ENTER KATE (YOUNG, REFINED, MIDDLE CLASS)

KATE. Hello. I'm Kate Portland-Brown. I'm supposed to audition for the part of Olypias.

PARTRIDGE. I'm Gill Partridge. Producer and director. And this is Jane Shannon. Authoress. She's a Keeper of Antiquities, whatever that may mean.

KATE. *(To Shannon)* How do you do?

SHANNON. Nice to meet you. Do call me Jane.

PARTRIDGE. *(Checking her CV)* You've only just left drama school.

KATE. One has to start somewhere.

PARTRIDGE. Olympias is the lead. Wife of King Philip. Bit of a nut case.

SHANNON. It's more complicated than that. She has never quite recovered from being initiated in the mystery cult of Dionysus –

PARTRIDGE. *(Brusquely)* She's a few buttons short of an overcoat. That's all the girl needs to know. *(To Kate)* I see you already have your script. Go back to your table, we'll call you when we're ready.

KATE. Thank you.

KATE EXITS

SHANNON. Not quite my idea of a Queen – or a Princess, come to that.

PARTRIDGE. We can't afford to be picky. *(Checks her CV's)* Who's next? Tatiana Verona. Not exactly a beginner. *(To audience)* Come in, Tatiana.

ENTER TATIANA (DRAMATIC AND FLAMBOYANT)

PARTRIDGE. Hello. I'm Gill Partridge. And this is the author, Jane Shannon.

TATIANA. *(To Shannon)* How do you do? It's a lovely script.

SHANNON. Oh, do you think so?

PARTRIDGE. Funny name yours. Tatiana Verona.

TATIANA. My dear mother was Russian. My awful father Italian. Heady mixture.

PARTRIDGE. So I see. *(Checking her CV)* You've been around a bit.

TATIANA. I have played Lady Macbeth.

PARTRIDGE. In Bognor.

TATIANA. And Mother Courage.

PARTRIDGE. In Runcorn.

TATIANA. I specialise in leading roles.

PARTRIDGE. Olympias is a big juicy part. Mad on snakes. Has them curling round her neck and scaring people to death.

TATIANA. I'm not keen on snakes. Is she bonkers?

SHANNON. Not really. Olympias is a female worshipper of Dionysus, the Greek god of nature's vital force.

TATIANA. Sex, you mean.

SHANNON. You could put it like that.

TATIANA. *(Enthusiastically)* Just my kind of part!

SHANNON. Olympias is wild, violent and headstrong.

TATIANA. A bit like Anne Widdicombe?

SHANNON. More so.

TATIANA. I can't wait to sink my teeth into it.

PARTRIDGE. Thank you, Tatiana, that'll be all for now.

TATIANA EXITS

SHANNON. Quite a character.

PARTRIDGE. Bit of a bossy boots. I don't like actors who try to think for themselves.

SHANNON. What about this Kate girl?

PARTRIDGE. What about her?

SHANNON. Where does she live?

PARTRIDGE. *(Checking)* South Kensington.

SHANNON. I don't know if she's quite right for the part of Olympias. Olympias was a gruesome old toughie. Mother of Alexander the Great.

PARTRIDGE. We'll try her as Eurydice. It's a lovely little part. King Philip gets rid of Olympias and remarries a docile local girl. Much more in Kate's line.

SHANNON. She then gets murdered by Olympias with her infant child.

PARTRIDGE. What do you think?

SHANNON. Just the right degree of naïve innocence.

PARTRIDGE. Then she's got the part.

SHANNON. And what about Tatiana?

PARTRIDGE. I daresay we better offer her a part before she's snapped up by the English National Opera. I hear they're recruiting tarts for Traviata.

SHANNON. She won't work with a real snake, you know.

PARTRIDGE. We'll mock something up.

SHANNON. I bet she's good at writhing.

PARTRIDGE. Let's just hope she doesn't slip a disc.

SHANNON. Shall we have her as Olympias then?

PARTRIDGE. *(Checking her notes)* I guess so. We've nobody else.

SHANNON. What about the men? We still need a King Philip and an Alexander the Great.

PARTRIDGE. There's two blokes outside. Brian Russell and Andrew Fraser. Let's wheel them in.

ENTER BRIAN (GENTLE, MIDDLE AGED) AND ANDREW (YOUNG AND SLIGHT)

BRIAN. Is this right? I'm supposed to read for King Philip of Macedon.

ANDREW. And I'm up for Alexander the Great.

PARTRIDGE. I'm the director. And this is the author. Did you come together?

BRIAN. No, we met on the staircase.

PARTRIDGE. I see you've both got scripts. I've marked the bits for you to read. You can have a quick look at them before we start.

ANDREW. Thank you.

PARTRIDGE. *(Checking her notes before turning to Brian)* Brian, there seems to be a gap of about twenty years in your CV. Were you resting all that time?

BRIAN. This is my second career.

PARTRIDGE. Oh, what was the first one?

BRIAN. Barclays Bank. I was in foreign exchange.

PARTRIDGE. *(To Andrew)* And what about you, Andrew?

ANDREW. I've just been in pantomime in Skegness. Simple Simon. But I prefer Chekhov.

PARTRIDGE. Mmmmm. *(To Shannon)* Will you take these two gentlemen away? I must speak to Tatiana.

SHANNON. Of course.

SHANNON EXITS WITH ANDREW AND BRIAN. ENTER TATIANA

PARTRIDGE. Congratulations. You're our leading lady.

TATIANA. That was quick. I didn't even audition.

PARTRIDGE. You don't have to. Talent shines.

TATIANA. Can I have my name above the title?

PARTRIDGE. No.

TATIANA. A taxi home each night?

PARTRIDGE. No.

TATIANA. I must at least have a new wig.

PARTRIDGE. I'll take you to the Oxfam Shop.

TATIANA. Haven't you got <u>any</u> funds for this show?

PARTRIDGE. They turned my theatre down for a grant. Said we weren't multi-ethnic enough. And we didn't have disabled access. That's all they care about. If I was to do a play about a lesbian black actress with a wooden leg, then the money would pour in.

TATIANA. *(Reading her script)* So, who's this bloke I'm married to?

PARTRIDGE. Philip is a warrior king. Dominates the Greeks. Got a grip on everyone. Except his own wife, Olympias. She's a bit of a wild one. So he ditches her.

TATIANA. What about this Alexander the Great? Do I get to be biblical with him?

PARTRIDGE. Alexander's as queer as a coot, dear. Everyone knows that.

TATIANA. But I thought he was a great general. Led his armies to many victories and shared in all their hardships.

PARTRIDGE. The grants people said we ought to appeal to minority tastes. Besides, there's money in the pink pound.

TATIANA. Are you paying Equity Minimum?

PARTRIDGE. Profit share.

TATIANA. I may have to withdraw, of course. I might get a call from the West End.

PARTRIDGE. We'll take the risk.

TATIANA EXITS. ENTER SHANNON

SHANNON. I'm a bit worried about the men. Philip and Alexander are supposed to be warrior kings. Brian looks decidedly mild and Andrew isn't exactly heroic.

PARTRIDGE. You can do a lot with lighting. I hope you're not going to keep piping up at rehearsals. Never address the actors except through me. It unsettles their tiny minds.

SHANNON. *(Peevish)* Oh, very well. But I do want every actor to be just right for the part.

PARTRIDGE. This isn't the National Theatre, you know.

SHANNON. There's one role you seem to have overlooked. The great philosopher Aristotle. Alexander's tutor. It may only be a small part but the actor needs to have enormous authority. Who's coming to read for that?

PARTRIDGE. I've cast it already.

SHANNON. Really? Who have you got?

PARTRIDGE. You'll see. It's my little secret.

SHANNON. Fair enough.

SHANNON EXITS

PARTRIDGE. *(Rings on her mobile)* Is that Phoenix Publishing? It's Gill Partridge here. I couldn't talk before. *(Pause)* Yes, I know you're in a hurry. But I told you already. We can't go ahead until – it happens. I'm as impatient as you are. In fact, I'm bloody desperate.

PARTRIDGE HANGS UP AND EXITS. ENTER SHANNON AND KATE

SHANNON. I'm afraid it's a bit grotty here.

KATE. Never mind. It's a real theatre.

SHANNON. Mad on acting, are you?

KATE. Mummy and Daddy don't approve. They think I'm going to meet undesirable people.

SHANNON. They'll be coming to see you perform?

KATE. Oh, yes. They always turned up for the tennis finals at school.

SHANNON. We'll have to get all our friends and family along, I'm afraid. It's the only way to drum up an audience on the fringe. Unless we get a good notice in *Time Out* or something. And they won't like this old fashioned stuff.

KATE. What's the point then?

SHANNON. To get seen. You only need one casting director to take a shine to you. That makes it all worth while.

KATE. Will we get casting directors out here?

SHANNON. You have to live in hope in this profession.

KATE. If you'll excuse me. I better go and practice my lines.

SHANNON. You do that.

KATE EXITS. ENTER PARTRIDGE

PARTRIDGE. I think everyone's here.

SHANNON. So what about Aristotle? We need to have somebody.

PARTRIDGE. I've already told you. I have somebody.

SHANNON. Who?

PARTRIDGE. Sir Emrys Merioneth.

SHANNON. Good God! He must be over a hundred.

PARTRIDGE. He's worked with all the greats. Gielgud. Olivier. He's only the most famous actor in the world. And the Greatest Living Welshman.

SHANNON. But young people only know him today through bit parts in Hollywood blockbusters. He was God in *Paradise Lost* with Leonardo di Caprio. He hasn't acted on stage for generations.

PARTRIDGE. This is going to be the making of us all. Sir Emrys Merioneth treads the boards again. The event of the year. And in your play! A dream come true.

SHANNON. How did you manage to get him?

PARTRIDGE. Never mind all that. He has honoured us all by agreeing to take part. So, it gives me great pleasure to introduce to you – Sir Emrys Merioneth.

ENTER EMRYS MERIONETH

SHANNON. Welcome, Sir Emrys. We're all tremendously glad to have you with us, sir. It's a huge honour for a fringe theatre. Tell me, what made you accept the part, sir?

EMRYS. Two reasons, I suppose. First, I've known Partridge here since she was a lass on the stage door of the Old Vic.

PARTRIDGE. That was my mother, sir.

EMRYS. It was in the late summer of '39. I was very young. I had my first great big success as Harry Hotspur. James Agate liked my legs. *(Pauses)* Something else happened at that time.

PARTRIDGE. They started a world war.

EMRYS. Thank you. I knew there was some other event. You've always followed my career with flattering interest. I think you know more about my achievements than I do myself. You must write my biography.

PARTRIDGE. Thank you, sir.

EMRYS. And the second reason? I liked the part of Aristotle. Not too many lines. My memory's not what it used to be. But enough to prove that I can represent the greatest brain the world has ever known. The critics, God damn them, have always alleged that I can only play brainless men of action. I want to show them that I can do intellectuals too.

SHANNON. How lucky for us.

EMRYS. And who are you?

PARTRIDGE. This is the author of the play.

EMRYS. It will need cutting. There are some wearisome bits between my appearances.

PARTRIDGE. Jane is quite prepared for that.

EMRYS. Let me say at once. I don't want any special treatment. I'll muck in just like anyone else. I shan't need a bath in my dressing room.

PARTRIDGE. Oh, good.

EMRYS. A shower will do. And a nice big couch. I rest for an hour before a performance. Totally alone.

PARTRIDGE. Well, actually – there's only one dressing room for the whole cast.

EMRYS. One dressing room? We all change together?

PARTRIDGE. This is the fringe, Sir Emrys.

EMRYS. Do you seriously expect me, a world famous star, to take off my trousers before – other actors?

PARTRIDGE. I –

EMRYS. That settles it. I was prepared to perform without pay. But I am not willing to strip naked before all and sundry. Kindly summon me a taxi. At the management's expense.

PARTRIDGE. I've got a solution. You must have the dressing room, Sir Emrys. The rest of the cast can share that little room in the basement.

EMRYS. All right. But I hope I'm not being a nuisance.

PARTRIDGE. Of course not. Now have you met all the cast?

EMRYS. Tell me about them before I meet them.

PARTRIDGE. We have Tatiana Verona. She's playing Olympias.

SHANNON. A woman of wild emotions and absolutely no self control.

PARTRIDGE. And we have Kate Portland-Brown as Eurydice.

EMRYS. Was that the young woman I met on the stairs?

PARTRIDGE. This is her first professional part.

EMRYS. How delightful. I shall monitor the young girl's progress with interest. *(Seductively)* I might even be able to give her a few tips.

PARTRIDGE. I'm sure she'll appreciate that, sir.

EMRYS. No need to call me sir. It makes me feel so old. Who else is in the cast?

PARTRIDGE. Brian Russell. He's Philip of Macedon.

EMRYS. Really?

PARTRIDGE. And Andrew Fraser. Alexander the Great.

EMRYS. *(Impatient)* Now, can we get going? I can't hang around here all day.

PARTRIDGE. Everyone's read the script.

SHANNON. In a nutshell, the play's a sensitive study of parental influence on a high-flying youth.

EMRYS. I hope you're not going to keep interrupting. The director's word is supreme. We should all listen to her with awe. Even me! Directors are often scared of me at first. But I encouraged them to be dictatorial. I welcome advice. Even criticism – occasionally!

PARTRIDGE. That's very encouraging, sir.

EMRYS. *(Checking his script)* Aristotle seems to fade out in the final scenes.

SHANNON. He's dead.

EMRYS. We need to develop that. We don't want the audience walking out before the end. Aristotle should have an affecting death scene. Very old and frail and learned. Perhaps he could be carried up to Olympus in a fiery chariot.

SHANNON. I doubt it.

PARTRIDGE. The play is already too long.

EMRYS. We could cut some of those scenes with Olympias.

SHANNON. I think Tatiana may have something to say about that.

EMRYS. I'm the one the public is coming to see. I don't want lots of lines but I must keep appearing.

PARTRIDGE. We'll talk about that, Sir Emrys. Perhaps we can make a start? We'll do Act One, Scene One. A magnificent apartment in the palace, richly decorated.

SHANNON. How on earth care we going to manage that?

PARTRIDGE. I've got some drapes left over from the pantomime.

EMRYS. *(Checking his watch)* Dear lady, have you seen the time? We need to take a break. We can pick this up after we have something to eat. I just hope the food here is edible.

EMRYS SWANS OFF

SHANNON. This is going to be pure hell. I think you've bitten off more than you can chew.

THEY EXIT

TWO

ENTER EMRYS, PARTRIDGE AND SHANNON

EMRYS. Damn it! I've forgotten my lines.

PARTRIDGE. Never mind, Sir Emrys. It'll be all right on the night.

SHANNON. I certainly hope so. The West End critics have booked in. Piranhas to a man.

EMRYS. While we've stopped, perhaps I could make a point. We've been rehearsing this play for ages and I don't feel we have it right. And as for the other actors, Brian sounds as if he's still issuing foreign currency at his bank. And as for Tatiana, she sounds like the head usherette at the Tottenham Scala. She's supposed to be worshipping the god of sex, not calling out bingo numbers.

SHANNON. *(Taking Partridge to one side)* Sir Emrys never stops attacking Tatiana. I don't think she can take any more. Either Sir Emrys goes or Tatiana goes.

PARTRIDGE. Don't be silly. You know that Sir Emrys is a tremendous asset to the show. He's so right for the part.

EMRYS. *(Interrupting)* And as for young Andrew, he's meant to be a world-beating hero. Just look at him. You'd take him for a peddler of cut-price pornography.

SHANNON. He's doing his best to appear manly. But since you've had most of his lines cut he's finding it very difficult.

EMRYS. *(To Partridge)* I do hope I'm not being a nuisance. You know the respect I always have for the director. But I <u>have</u> worked with the biggest names in the business. I used to play tennis with Cary Grant.

SHANNON. *(Hands Emrys a piece of parchment)* Here's that extra speech you asked for, Sir Emrys. Aristotle is musing among the royal tombs. To get round the learning difficulty, I thought you might like to read it from a parchment.

EMRYS. Won't the tombs be dark?

SHANNON. You could have a candle in the other hand.

EMRYS. Sounds tricky.

PARTRIDGE. We'll try it after the break.

EMRYS. Must have a pee first.

EMRYS EXITS

SHANNON. Horrible old Welsh windbag!

PARTRIDGE. He's brought us a huge advance booking.

SHANNON. I'm going to make an image of Sir Emrys and stick pins into his private parts.

PARTRIDGE. Not until the show is over, please.

SHANNON. I'm sorry, I have to say it. Sir Emrys is perfectly ghastly.

PARTRIDGE. He's a national treasure.

SHANNON. Then he should be in a museum. Did you know he would be so appalling?

PARTRIDGE. I thought he would be worth the gamble.

SHANNON. You know an awful lot about him, don't you?

PARTRIDGE. I've studied him for years. His public life. And also his private. His life has been a passion of mine. I could write a book on the man.

SHANNON. I must say, you do seem very patient with the old monster. Always enquiring after his health. He's not going to peg out on us, is he?

PARTRIDGE. He'll outlive the both of us. He just likes to be the focus of attention.

SHANNON. He's ruining my play. He won't let you direct it. He's infuriating the other actors. Tatiana's at boiling point most of the time. He can't remember his own lines. We'll get a roasting from the critics.

PARTRIDGE. Bad notices are better than no notices.

SHANNON. I've been researching this play for years. Gave up everything for it. My summer holidays with mother. Even the Museum Croquet Championship.

PARTRIDGE. Perhaps you need a break from rehearsals.

SHANNON. Oh, no. I have to be here. There's a certain macabre fascination in seeing one's work mangled before one's very own eyes. Like undergoing open-heart surgery with only a local anaesthetic.

PARTRIDGE. You'll just have to grin and bear it. A playwright needs the hide of a rhinoceros, combined with the patience of a saint. Now, I must find Brian. He wanted a word with me. Why don't you go and grab a coffee?

SHANNON EXITS. ENTER BRIAN

BRIAN. I'd like a quick word with you.

PARTRIDGE. What's the matter, Brian?

BRIAN. I've decided to give up acting. It isn't for me.

PARTRIDGE. What will you do instead?

BRIAN. I've applied for one of those jobs as a tour guide. You go around London in an open-topped bus, telling Americans when you get to St Paul's.

PARTRIDGE. Sounds like hard work.

BRIAN. It's quite easy to spot St Paul's. And you get a free lunch at a Burger King – with a diet coke thrown in.

PARTRIDGE. Don't act rashly, Brian. Just because you've been put off by those silly remarks from the old boy.

BRIAN. He sees me as a figure of fun. Continually reminding me that I'm meant to be a warrior king. It's not my fault I've got thin arms.

PARTRIDGE. Take no notice. The man's not worked on the fringe before. We have to bring him down to our level.

ENTER EMRYS

EMRYS. What are you two chatting about?

PARTRIDGE. Well, since you ask, Sir Emrys, Brian was telling me that he's been discouraged by some of your comments.

EMRYS. Discouraged? You astonish me. I've always enjoyed excellent relations with the rest of the cast. I used to have tremendous romps with Dame Edith and Dame Sybil.

BRIAN. I'm not asking for romps, just common courtesy.

EMRYS. We must put this right at once. I don't like to leave anyone with bad thoughts about me, however humble they may be. In case I die in the night. Leave us, Partridge, I want a word with Brian.

PARTRIDGE. All right.

PARTRIDGE EXITS

EMRYS. Now, let's have this out. I may have seemed a tiny bit critical. It's my high standards. You get like that, working with Larry and Noel and Johnny G. But I think you have promise. You'll develop into quite a competent actor.

BRIAN. *(Coldly)* Thank you.

EMRYS. You'll never be a star, of course.

BRIAN. Oh, really. How does one get to be a star?

EMRYS. You don't. Stars are born. It's a matter of personal magnetism. When a star is on stage, nobody notices anyone else.

BRIAN. Rather hard on the others.

EMRYS. They get used to it. The important thing is to look different from the rest of the human race. You need to be either conspicuously beautiful or else dramatically ugly.

BRIAN. *(Nastily)* Which are you?

EMRYS. The former. *(Kindly)* Look, I'm sorry if I seemed unkind.

BRIAN. *(Slightly mollified)* Thank you, Sir Emrys. I appreciate that.

EMRYS. Is there something I can do for you? I heard you on the phone earlier. Something about money – you seemed a little flustered -

BRIAN. Well, there is one thing. I hardly like to mention it.

EMRYS. Go on, dear boy.

BRIAN. I am very short of money. I did get a small pay-off from the bank, but I used that on a rash investment. And now I'm desperate to buy my flat.

EMRYS. No problem. I'll write you a cheque. Come to my dressing room.

BRIAN. That's tremendously good of you, sir. It would only be a short-term loan, of course. I could give you an IOU in writing.

EMRYS. No need for that. An understanding between gentlemen.

BRIAN. I'm very grateful.

EMRYS. *(Looking around)* Seeing I'm in an apologetic mood, where is that Kate girl? I daresay I owe her an apology as well. Would you go and fetch her for me? And don't worry about the money. Us thespians must stick together.

BRIAN EXITS. ENTER KATE

EMRYS. Ah, my dear, a word. I wanted to tell you, you're doing very well.

KATE. *(Delighted)* Oh, thank you, Sir Emrys.

EMRYS. Just call me Emrys. You're very attractive, you know. I predict for you a great career on the stage.

KATE. I wish you'd say that to Mummy and Daddy.

EMRYS. I will. When I have the pleasure of meeting them.

KATE. You're very kind.

EMRYS. I like to bring on the young. I'll tell you what, why don't you come along to my dressing room for a drop of brandy? We could have a really nice chat?

KATE. I should love that. Can I bring Mummy?

EMRYS. No. You may not bring Mummy. I want you all on my own. I shall show you some of my scrapbooks. A pictorial record of my long career. All those lunches by the pool in Bel Air – with Clark Gable and Joan Crawford and Bette Davies. My salad days when I was young and lovely.

KATE. You still look very distinguished.

EMRYS. Thank you, my dear. You're the sweetest girl. We are already great friends, and we shall be even more so.

KATE. You are so kind.

EMRYS. One tries to spread a little happiness. Now, please, I must leave you. I have to read through a new speech handed to me by our tame author.

KATE. You haven't seen Andrew, have you?

EMRYS. No, I haven't.

KATE. I wonder where he is?

EMRYS. I must depart, my dear.

EMRYS EXITS. ENTER PARTRIDGE AND ANDREW

PARTRIDGE. Don't be long, you two. It's time for a dress rehearsal.

ANDREW. *(To Kate)* Am I interrupting anything?

KATE. Sir Emrys has been very encouraging.

ANDREW. Has he now? You just keep away from him.

KATE. Why should I? He's a lovely old man. He's asked me to join him for a drink.

ANDREW. I'll bet.

KATE. He's going to show me his album of rare photos.

ANDREW. You watch out.

KATE. But he's so old. Surely that instinct dies as men get older?

ANDREW. Not a bit of it. They just get more desperate. He'll be taking Viagra, you know.

KATE. I think you're just jealous.

ANDREW. I just don't want some old man pawing you.

KATE. Thank you, Andrew, I can take care of myself.

PARTRIDGE. Come along, you two. It's time for a dress rehearsal. Off you go. Now, where is that Tatiana woman?

KATE AND ANDREW EXIT. ENTER TATIANA

PARTRIDGE. Come along, Tatiana.

TATIANA. Can you give me a moment?

PARTRIDGE. What is it now?

TATIANA. It's my costume.

PARTRIDGE. What about it?

TATIANA. The trouble is – I simply can't do a lascivious dance in what you've given me. I need to wriggle and display my attractions.

PARTRIDGE. Then take it off.

TATIANA. I'm supposed to be Queen of Macedon. Do you expect me to prance around in my bra and pants? I'll require a nice simple undergarment. In silk. Like they have in the Royal Ballet.

PARTRIDGE. Tatiana, this is a dress rehearsal. The phone is jammed with callers trying to book seats. I have to concentrate on the big picture. I simply can't be bothered with your little problem.

TATIANA. My little problem! There's only one costume per actor. And I have to wear a sack cloth?

PARTRIDGE. Okay, okay, let's have a look in the wardrobe.

TATIANA. And another thing, I'm going to find it a great strain taking four buses home every night. I'd like you to reconsider your decision not to pay for a taxi for me. After all, you'll be shelling out for Sir Emrys.

PARTRIDGE. He's famous. And fragile. He suffers from high blood pressure, you know.

TATIANA. I may not be famous – yet. But I'm certainly fragile. You'll be coining money with these big audiences.

PARTRIDGE. There's a lot of debt to pay off. It was a mistake doing that all-male *Romeo and Juliet* as a Christmas show.

TATIANA. Don't mind me then. I'm only your leading lady. I'm off!

PARTRIDGE. You certainly are, dear!

TATIANA EXITS. ENTER SHANNON

SHANNON. Ah, there you are. A word. I'm really worried about Sir Emrys. Where is he, by the way?

PARTRIDGE. I don't know. I expect he's having a sleep.

SHANNON. I know he's an asset at the box office, but he's wrecking my play.

PARTRIDGE. He has tremendous authority on stage.

SHANNON. That's no use, he can't remember the lines. The only ones he gets right are the ones he has to read. The others – he makes up – and not very well at that.

PARTRIDGE. I'm sorry, you'll just have to lump it.

SHANNON. Mother is coming to the first night. And the ancient historians too. This could damage my career at the museum.

PARTRIDGE. *(Ignoring Shannon)* Do you think we could have the whole cast on stage? Where's Brian?

ENTER BRIAN

BRIAN. Don't you think I ought to have a sword and a helmet with my costume? After all, I did conquer the whole of Greece.

PARTRIDGE. We'll see, we'll see.

BRIAN. Have you seen Sir Emrys?

PARTRIDGE. What am I, his keeper?

BRIAN. *(Upset)* He's really upset me. He's gone back on his word. He wants his cheque back. I've already paid a deposit on my flat. He must have realised that. It was a cruel trick. *(Loud)* I could murder the swine!

PARTRIDGE. Now, where <u>are</u> the others? Kate. Andrew. Where are you?

ENTER KATE AND ANDREW

KATE. I suppose he's asleep in his dressing room, the wicked old fraud.

ANDREW. I thought you adored him.

KATE. Not any longer. Not after just now. I thought he just wanted to show me his photos, but he didn't. I hate telling you. He started using revolting words and tried taking my clothes off.

ANDREW. Disgusting!

KATE. When he could see I wasn't having it, he turned nasty. Said he would wreck my career.

ANDREW. I did tell you. The Welsh are over-sexed.

KATE. You were right. What are we to do now? Other girls ought to be warned.

ANDREW. We'll get our revenge.

KATE. Shall we tell the police?

ANDREW. Be careful. If they decide to prosecute, you'd be called as a witness.

KATE. Daddy and Mummy would hate that. They were awfully upset when Aunt Cressida was fined for speeding.

ANDREW. You know how malicious people are. You know what people say - no smoke without fire.

KATE. How horrible.

ANDREW. There's a better way. I'll beat him up. It will be a pleasure. After all his remarks about my physique.

KATE. Be careful. You might kill him.

ANDREW. I'd like to – this has made me mad.

KATE. That's rather sweet of you. I can see – you really care.

ANDREW. Of course I care.

KATE. I can't think why.

ANDREW. Yes, you can, you silly girl.

PARTRIDGE AND SHANNON MOVE FORWARD

SHANNON. Couldn't we stick his lines onto the back of the furniture? That's what they did for Ellen Terry in old age.

PARTRIDGE. Now, where are the actors? I want to get started. *(The actors move forward. Partridge calls order)* Can I have your attention please! We need to start the dress rehearsal. Now, where is Sir Emrys?

ENTER SIR EMRYS, STABBED IN THE CHEST. HE FALLS AND DIES

PARTRIDGE. Sir Emrys. *(She examines him)*

SHANNON. What's the matter with him?

PARTRIDGE. It's his heart.

SHANNON. What, a heart attack?

PARTRIDGE. No, he's been stabbed in the chest. Straight into the heart.

SHANNON. *(To everyone)* Come on, everyone. Help me get Sir Emrys off stage.

THEY ALL EXIT

FADE

THREE

ENTER PARTRIDGE AND SHANNON

PARTRIDGE. We've got to keep calm.

SHANNON. How can we keep calm? With the police here to question us all. I've already met the bloke in charge. Chap called Gloat.

PARTRIDGE. Detective Inspector Harold <u>Stoat</u>. Sounds like a name invented by some third rate crime writer.

SHANNON. I bet Stoat's a stage name. He wants to get us all transfixed like a pack of frightened rabbits.

PARTRIDGE. Who on earth would have a motive for killing Sir Emrys?

SHANNON. It's quite a long list, actually. Take Kate, for example. Sir Emrys was a dirty old man towards her. That would give her a first class motive for sticking the knife in. And don't forget Andrew. He was awfully cross with Sir Emrys for compromising young Kate's honour.

PARTRIDGE. There's also Tatiana. She wasn't exactly close to Sir Emrys. And as for Brian, there's money involved there somewhere.

SHANNON. And what about the play? We can't go on now.

PARTRIDGE. Ah, but we have got something better than the play. Notoriety. We're all going to be famous.

SHANNON. This evening should have been wonderful. The house sold out. Mother in the front row. The West End critics here in force. Myself acclaimed as the new Jeffrey Archer. And what have we got instead? The police tramping around in their size twelves.

PARTRIDGE. Don't worry. We'll still get your play on.

SHANNON. Who are we going to get to replace Sir Emrys? You kept on telling me he was a massive star with huge appeal –

PARTRIDGE. As he often reminded us.

SHANNON. This is just my luck. I've always had bad luck. My fiancée left me for the Keeper of Ancient Artefacts, you know. He said that ancient artefacts were more fun than me.

ENTER INSPECTOR STOAT

PARTRIDGE. Ah, Inspector Stoat.

STOAT. I'd like to say again, how very sorry I am for you all that your play has had to be postponed.

PARTRIDGE. Only for forty-eight hours. I'm rehearsing a new Aristotle tomorrow. It's a short part, though Sir Emrys made it seem enormous.

STOAT. There may be other parts to fill too.

PARTRIDGE. What do you mean, Inspector?

STOAT. You cannot rely on having all your present cast available – if there had to be an arrest. However, I do hope to conclude my investigation very quickly. We have already done our forensics. And we can now be virtually certain that no outside person entered the theatre, which allows us to narrow down the suspects.

PARTRIDGE. The suspects being –

STOUT. Everyone in this company. Now, I'm not making any accusations – yet.

SHANNON. What about the knife, Inspector? Aren't there any fingerprints? DNA traces?

STOUT. That is one of the least satisfactory aspects of this case. After the murder was discovered, everyone rushed around the scene of the crime in disarray –

SHANNON. Like scalded hens, more like.

STOAT. That confusion allowed someone – presumably the murderer – to draw out the knife and make off with it – leaving a lot of blood but no weapon.

PARTRIDGE. But someone should have stopped him –

SHANNON. Or her.

STOAT. Indeed, they should. But that sort of thing only happens in detective stories, where there is always some superior person, like Monsieur Poirot, to take immediate charge.

SHANNON. *(To Partridge)* Why didn't you take charge?

PARTRIDGE. I have no experience of murder.

STOAT. Never mind all that. I am not easily baffled. The other classic line of enquiry is through the analysis of motive. I shall need to speak to each member of the company individually.

PARTRIDGE. We've already given a lot of details to your Sergeant.

STOAT. I shall supplement that. By training my mental searchlight.

PARTRIDGE. Come again.

STOAT. The capacity to feel with immense accuracy through the tips of the fingers. Some of us have it, others don't. *(To the audience)* Now, let me warn you all. Do not attempt to conceal anything from me. I am a trained investigator. I have been though the Interpol Summer School – not to mention the FBI Advanced Correspondence Course.

PARTRIDGE. So, who's first on your list, Inspector?

STOAT. I shall speak with Tatiana Verona.

PARTRIDGE. I'll fetch her for you.

STOAT. And you can leave us in peace.

PARTRIDGE AND SHANNON EXIT. ENTER TATIANA

STOAT. Do come in, Doris.

TATIANA. Doris?

STOAT. That's your real name, isn't it? Doris Postlethwaite?

TATIANA. I don't use my real name. It's so lower middle class. Call me Tatiana – or darling, for short.

STOAT. Well, Tatiana, I would like you to tell me about your relationship with the victim.

TATIANA. We were very close.

STOAT. Be more precise, please. Did you indulge in heavy petting, the full monty or kinky variations?

TATIANA. Really, Inspector. You rather shock me. Sir Emrys was well stricken in years. Somewhat past it, in fact.

STOAT. So what drew you to each other, then? Was it his admiration for your acting ability?

TATIANA. That certainly helped. It was flattering to be admired by a great star. He liked my bravura, as he used to call it.

STOAT. Are you sure you're not telling me a porky?

TATIANA. Perfectly sure.

STOAT. *(Taking out a diary)* Then how do you account for these entries in Sir Emrys' diary? We found it in his dressing room. **"Another ghastly rehearsal. That hideous cow who calls herself Tatiana is ruining everything with her grotesque over-acting. I long to plant a kick on her overblown rump."** There is a lot more in the same vein.

TATIANA. How very wounding. I didn't know he was keeping a diary.

STOAT. Nobody did. A bit of luck for us. It now seems that this was his main motive for taking the part. He had secured a substantial advance for it from a publisher.

TATIANA. The malicious old bastard!

STOAT. Murder victims often are.

TATIANA. If you must know, Sir Emrys was absolutely bloody to me. He kept criticising my performance in front of the others.

STOAT. You hated him?

TATIANA. I certainly did.

STOAT. The truth at last. It always comes out, under expert professional probing. But did you hate him enough to murder him?

TATIANA. Yes. *(Pause)* But I didn't.

STOAT. Why should I believe you?

TATIANA. Because I aim for a future in show business – not in some God-forsaken prison – with Lord Longford as my only visitor.

STOAT. Lord Longford is long dead.

TATIANA. Do you think that would stop him?

STOAT. I think you could be a great hater.

TATIANA. If I killed everyone who had done me harm, there would be a terrible mortality amongst casting directors.

STOAT. We'll leave it at that then – for the time being.

TATIANA. You will keep my secret, won't you?

STOAT. What secret?

TATIANA. About being called Doris.

STOAT. As you leave, do ask Kate Portland-Brown to come in. And don't go too far.

TATIANA. I never go too far – except on purpose.

STOAT. Just ask Miss Portland-Brown to come in.

TATIANA EXITS. ENTER KATE

KATE. I'm so sorry, Inspector. I just couldn't bear the suspense any longer. I kept waiting to be called. It was an agony. I'm on the verge of collapse.

STOAT. This won't take long.

KATE. I do hope I'm not being a nuisance. Andrew and I were trying to go through our lines. But I couldn't remember mine. It was like being back at school.

STOAT. So, you feel guilty?

KATE. Not guilty. Agitated. Can't you tell the difference?

STOAT. I ask the questions around here. Now, Miss Portland-Brown. What were your relations like with the late Sir Emrys?

KATE. I was very fond of the old gentleman. And I was greatly honoured to be in the play with him.

STOAT. Is that so?

KATE. Oh, yes. He seemed to take an interest in me.

STOAT. A professional interest?

KATE. He said he would make me into a big star.

STOAT. How was he proposing to do that?

KATE. By giving me private coaching.

STOAT. In the privacy of his dressing room?

KATE. Yes.

STOAT. Tell me, did Sir Emrys, on any occasion, ever make any improper suggestions?

KATE. No. He was always very sweet. Very much a gentleman.

STOAT. So, your memories of the late Sir Emrys are totally happy?

KATE. Yes.

STOAT. Miss Portland-Brown, you may be young but you are already highly accomplished -

KATE. Thank you, Inspector.

STOAT. A highly accomplished liar.

KATE. No!

STOAT. Yes!

KATE. *(Breaks down)* I knew I should have come clean. I wanted to tell the truth right from the start.

STOAT. Never under-rate the force, Miss Portland-Brown. And me in particular. You see, I am ahead of you. I have possession of the diary kept by Sir Emrys from the moment he accepted the role of Aristotle until the moment of his death. Allow me to read a few choice extracts. **"That tasty young Kate has made me feel quite randy again. I am grateful to her for that. She has certainly got my imagination going. How I long to fondle those deliciously rounded breasts and pert buttocks.**

KATE. How disgusting!

STOAT. There's more. **"I decoyed young Kate into my dressing room earlier. Opened a bottle of my best brandy. We sat on the sofa holding hands and listened to some Tchaikovsky. She kept staring at me mistily out of those pretty blue eyes. I could not make out whether she was short-sighted, deeply in love or just badly in need of a poke. I decided to chance the full frontal approach. That used to work so well with Ava Gardner. Murmuring words of encouragement, I flung myself upon the appetising filly and started to simplify her clothing. She flushed scarlet, jumped up screaming and fled through the door shouting something of a threatening nature about Daddy. A pity! She could have learned a lot from an old master."**

KATE. The swine!

STOAT. Did Andrew Fraser know about this?

KATE. I did tell Andrew. He was horrified.

STOAT. So you planned revenge.

KATE. I never said that.

STOAT. You didn't have to. Will you fetch Andrew Fraser?

KATE EXITS. ENTER ANDREW

ANDREW. I heard all that. That was his own guilty conscience speaking. I may have scowled at him. But Kate had only told me about his disgusting behaviour just before he died.

STOAT. You never liked his attitude towards Kate.

ANDREW. We both hated the old brute. But that was all. I may talk tough on occasion. But I was only psyching myself up to play Alexander the Great. But really, I'm as gentle as a lamb.

STOAT. It is quite possible to be savaged by sheep. As Lady Thatcher discovered.

ANDREW. My intentions may have been murderous, but someone else got there first.

STOAT. You do have a record of violence. Two years ago you were arrested in a basement club in Soho.

ANDREW. A minor punch-up. He was rude about Chelsea.

STOAT. The charge was not proceeded with. But it is an indication of your character.

ANDREW. So, you're arresting me.

STOAT. You can go now – for the time being.

ANDREW. Shall I send in the next victim?

STOAT. Victim? I think you mean the next person for interview. We have sensitive, humane policing these days. It's the latest gimmick.

ANDREW. So, who do you want to speak to next?

STOAT. Brian Russell.

ANDREW EXITS. ENTER BRIAN

STOAT. Come in, Mr Russell. I suppose you're going to try and bamboozle me too.

BRIAN. What on earth do you mean, Inspector?

STOAT. Everyone's trying to tell me that Sir Emrys was such a delightful old man.

BRIAN. Well, he was. I became very fond of him.

STOAT. I am not deceived by your urbane manner, no doubt cultivated at the bank as you turned down overdrafts and foreclosed on mortgages.

BRIAN. Actually I sold lire, deutchmarks, francs, pesetas – that is, until they brought in the Euro.

STOAT. An activity you must have found wearisome.

BRIAN. Indeed.

STOAT. But you concealed your feelings. For the sake of good customer relations.

BRIAN. I suppose so.

STOAT. So you are used to - masking your emotions.

BRIAN. It's all part of the job.

STOAT. Are you drawing on that skill now? To project yourself as an admirer of the late Sir Emrys, whereas I happen to know that you are secretly delighted at his sudden death.

BRIAN. How do you know that?

STOAT. We have read his diary. He states quite explicitly that he offered you a large sum of money. And, hours before his death, he went back on his word.

BRIAN. I don't deny that. He treated me abominably. He went back on his word. It was a trick to make a fool of me.

STOAT. But you made a fool of him, didn't you? In the end. You had his cheque in his hand. His executors would have to honour the agreement.

BRIAN. That's my good luck.

STOAT. It also gave you a strong motive for killing him.

BRIAN. Maybe, but I didn't do it. I'm too cautious to make a killer. Why do you think I slaved away in that damned bank all those years?

STOAT. But you left?

BRIAN. A machine replaced me.

STOAT. I see. Thank you, Mr Russell. That will do.

BRIAN. I'm free to go?

STOAT. Wait with the others please. And send in Jane Shannon.

BRIAN. *(Disappointed)* Aren't you interested in my background, Inspector? My psychology? What makes me tick?

STOAT. No.

BRIAN. I was expecting an in-depth interview.

STOAT. I'm too busy.

BRIAN. A pity. Nobody's ever been interested in me.

BRIAN EXITS. ENTER SHANNON

SHANNON. What a disaster. Mother was so looking forward to it.

STOAT. Were you satisfied with the production?

SHANNON. Oh, yes. It was so terribly exciting to hear my words spoken by real professional actors.

STOAT. And you were pleased with Sir Emrys?

SHANNON. He was superb. That enormous dignity.

STOAT. What of his lines? I gather it can be a problem with older performers.

SHANNON. He was fine. Tonight would have been a triumph. You probably won't understand this, Inspector, but we playwrights are a vulnerable breed. You deliver your precious work. Then you have to share it with others. A bruising experience.

ENTER PARTRIDGE

PARTRIDGE. Sorry to barge in. But how long this will all take.

STOAT. I don't think I need to bother Miss Shannon any longer.

SHANNON EXITS

PARTRIDGE. So, what do you make of our authoress?

STOAT. She's out of the frame. Absolutely no motive. Rather the reverse. She needed the great actor to remain alive. To add lustre to her play.

PARTRIDGE. Do you think she was really satisfied with Sir Emrys' performance?

STOAT. She told me so herself.

PARTRIDGE. Oh, did she?

STOAT. What do you mean?

PARTRIDGE. I'd rather not say.

STOAT. It's your duty to help me. This is a murder enquiry.

PARTRIDGE. All right. Jane Shannon was fed up with Sir Emrys. The old boy was disrupting rehearsals. And he couldn't learn his lines. He was making Shannon's play sound ridiculous. You can imagine what that would mean to an author.

STOAT. Then she's a suspect too. Oh dear, it's all so complicated. The truth is that Sir Emrys was universally disliked. They all had a motive for killing the poor man.

PARTRIDGE. Perhaps they organised it together?

STOAT. Hardly likely. That only happens in Agatha Christie novels.

PARTRIDGE. Am I also a suspect?

STOAT. Certainly not! You did have a motive, but it was for keeping the old gentleman alive. He's brought you enormous advance bookings.

PARTRIDGE. They were paying to see a living legend in the flesh.

STOAT. So, you're badly out of pocket?

PARTRIDGE. Yes.

STOAT. Shame you couldn't benefit from the old boy's death.

PARTRIDGE. How could I?

STOAT. You've known him for a long time. You could have written his life story.

PARTRIDGE. *(Starts to wriggle)*

STOAT. Miss Partridge, I didn't know I had that effect on you.

PARTRIDGE. *(Takes out a mobile phone)* Don't flatter yourself, Inspector. My phone's on vibrate. *(She answers the phone)* Sorry, can't talk to you now. *(hangs up)*

STOAT. At least you're in the clear.

PARTRIDGE. That's a relief.

STOAT. It means I can talk freely to you. In confidence. One requires contact with the average mind. Every Sherlock Holmes needs his Doctor Watson. Now, you know the suspects better than I do. Which one would you consider the front runner?

PARTRIDGE. Tatiana of course. She's the only one with the guts to do it. The only problem is lack of proof.

STOAT. The police don't often let lack of proof stand in the way of a conviction.

PARTRIDGE. So, how do we solve this particular case?

STOAT. Criminals tend to betray themselves in the end. Stoat of the Yard doesn't handle many unsolved cases. But first, we must break for coffee.

THEY EXIT

FADE

FOUR

ENTER PARTRIDGE AND SHANNON

PARTRIDGE. We'll break there. Where's the new Aristotle?

SHANNON. He's in the dressing room. Learning his lines.

PARTRIDGE. Let him be. We open tomorrow.

SHANNON. It won't be the same.

PARTRIDGE. We'll have a good house. Instead of the drama critics, we'll be full of crime reporters.

SHANNON. What's happened to Inspector Gloat?

PARTRIDGE. Stoat. He'll be here any minute.

SHANNON. What's this I hear about your book? Mother heard it on the news.

PARTRIDGE. Oh, that.

SHANNON. Oh, that nothing. Mother said you've signed a contract with a publisher. For some huge amount. A life of Sir Emrys Merioneth. No holds barred apparently.

PARTRIDGE. I've still got to bring it up to date. When we know who killed him.

SHANNON. Congratulations anyway. This is bound to make you very rich.

PARTRIDGE. I do have huge debts to clear.

SHANNON. But there'll still be enough over to pay the actors Equity Minimum.

PARTRIDGE. Perhaps.

SHANNON. You were always interested in Sir Emrys.

PARTRIDGE. Meeting him was one of the big thrills of my youth. I've collected quite a dossier.

SHANNON. About his private life?

PARTRIDGE. Of course. It's going to be the show business sensation of the year.

SHANNON. You couldn't have published all this stuff while the old boy was still alive.

PARTRIDGE. Well, he isn't, is he?

Murder Mysteries Vol 2

ENTER STOAT

STOAT. Evening, everyone. *(To Partridge)* I understand congratulations are in order. Your new book. I daresay I shall figure in the last chapter.

PARTRIDGE. Indeed you will, Inspector.

STOAT. You must have been working on it for years, to be able to produce it so soon.

PARTRIDGE. It's been a bit of an obsession. He was one of the great actors of the century. And ever since he worked with my mother during the war -

SHANNON. On stage and screen.

PARTRIDGE. And in bed.

SHANNON. Should be a juicy read. I'm dying to get hold of a copy.

PARTRIDGE. *(Produces a manuscript which she hands to Shannon)* You can glance through this manuscript, if you like.

SHANNON. *(To Stoat)* What about the murder enquiry, Inspector?

STOAT. Thank you. I was almost forgetting that. In all the excitement.

SHANNON. Are you planning on making an arrest?

STOAT. I always make an arrest. *(Feebly)* Or nearly always. It's simply a question of finding the right person.

SHANNON. You have a prime suspect?

STOAT. Indeed, I do.

SHANNON. *(Handing back the manuscript to Partridge)* I'll read this later. I won't be able to concentrate at the moment. *(A letter falls out of the manuscript. Stoat picks it up as Shannon exits)*

PARTRIDGE. Excuse me, Inspector. That's my letter.

STOAT. So I see.

PARTRIDGE. It's got nothing to do with your enquiry.

STOAT. If you don't mind, anything to do with the victim could be relevant to my investigation. *(Opening Partridge's letter)* Ah, this is very interesting. A copy of a letter addressed to your publisher's solicitors. Two weeks ago. From a QC in the Temple. A specialist in the law of libel. He advises that it would be a great mistake to publish your life of Sir Emrys while the great actor was still alive.

PARTRIDGE. So?

STOAT. So? This means that you had an excellent motive for wishing Sir Emrys dead. I think you'd better explain.

PARTRIDGE. *(Giving in)* It was so unfair. I'd based all my plans on the assumption that the old bugger would have popped his clogs years ago. I was desperate for the money. But the old sod just went on and on. It was so annoying. He was in the pink of condition.

STOAT. So you decided to do something about it.

PARTRIDGE. I enlisted him for this bloody play in the hope that the exertion would finish him off. But he seemed to thrive on it. The rest you can guess.

STOAT. There we have it. One more murder solved.

PARTRIDGE. Except for one thing, Inspector. You haven't got much evidence against me.

STOAT. Oh yes I have. You've just made a full confession.

PARTRIDGE. You have no witnesses. I shall say you made it all up. It's not as if you have a tape recorder or anything.

STOAT. Maybe not, but I do have an audience to back me up.

PARTRIDGE. *(Looking out over the audience)* I wouldn't bank on that lot to back a winner in a one-horse race.

STOAT. I'm not going to. It's this lot I'm banking on.

ENTER THE WHOLE CAST

SHANNON. We heard it all. And we have good memories – being actors and writers.

PARTRIDGE. I'll get you all expelled from Equity for this.

SHANNON. You won't get anyone expelled – not where you're going.

PARTRIDGE. Oh, and where will that be?

SHANNON. Beyond the fringe, dear girl. Beyond the fringe.

THEY ALL TAKE A BOW AND EXIT

END OF PLAY

Printed in Great Britain
by Amazon

45056218R00061